Updates and Commentary in Public International Law, 2019

Updates and Commentary in Public International Law, 2019

Anastasia Telesetsky
Professor of Law
University of Idaho College of Law

ASPEN
PUBLISHING

To contact Customer Service, e-mail customer.service@aspenpublishing.com, call 1-800-950-5259, or mail correspondence to:

Aspen Publishing
Attn: Order Department
PO Box 990
Frederick, MD 21705

Printed in the United States of America.

1 2 3 4 5 6 7 8 9 0

ISBN 978-1-5438-1370-8

About Aspen Publishing

Aspen Publishing is a leading provider of educational content and digital learning solutions to law schools in the U.S. and around the world. Aspen provides best-in-class solutions for legal education through authoritative textbooks, written by renowned authors, and breakthrough products such as Connected eBooks, Connected Quizzing, and PracticePerfect.

The Aspen Casebook Series (famously known among law faculty and students as the "red and black" casebooks) encompasses hundreds of highly regarded textbooks in more than eighty disciplines, from large enrollment courses, such as Torts and Contracts to emerging electives such as Sustainability and the Law of Policing. Study aids such as the *Examples & Explanations* and the *Emanuel Law Outlines* series, both highly popular collections, help law students master complex subject matter.

Major products, programs, and initiatives include:

- **Connected eBooks** are enhanced digital textbooks and study aids that come with a suite of online content and learning tools designed to maximize student success. Designed in collaboration with hundreds of faculty and students, the Connected eBook is a significant leap forward in the legal education learning tools available to students.

- **Connected Quizzing** is an easy-to-use formative assessment tool that tests law students' understanding and provides timely feedback to improve learning outcomes. Delivered through CasebookConnect.com, the learning platform already used by students to access their Aspen casebooks, Connected Quizzing is simple to implement and integrates seamlessly with law school course curricula.

- **PracticePerfect** is a visually engaging, interactive study aid to explain commonly encountered legal doctrines through easy-to-understand animated videos, illustrative examples, and numerous practice questions. Developed by a team of experts, PracticePerfect is the ideal study companion for today's law students.

- The **Aspen Learning Library** enables law schools to provide their students with access to the most popular study aids on the market across all of their courses. Available through an annual subscription, the online library consists of study aids in e-book, audio, and video formats with full text search, note-taking, and highlighting capabilities.

- Aspen's **Digital Bookshelf** is an institutional-level online education bookshelf, consolidating everything students and professors need to ensure success. This program ensures that every student has access to affordable course materials from day one.

- **Leading Edge** is a community centered on thinking differently about legal education and putting those thoughts into actionable strategies. At the core of the program is the Leading Edge Conference, an annual gathering of legal education thought leaders looking to pool ideas and identify promising directions of exploration.

Contents

Acknowledgments

The author gratefully acknowledges the following sources, which granted permission to reprint excerpts from the works listed below:

Dejusticia, Excerpts from Corte Suprema de Justicia, Sala de Casación Civil (April 4, 2018), English translation. Copyright © 2018 by Dejusticia. Reprinted by permission. All rights reserved.

Inter-American Court of Human Rights, "Request for an Advisory Opinion Presented by the Government of the Republic of Ecuador to the Inter-American Court of Human Rights Concerning the Scope and Purpose of the Right of Asylum in Light of International Human Rights Law, Inter-American Law, and International Law" (2016). Copyright © 2016 by the Inter-American Court of Human Rights. Reprinted by permission. All rights reserved.

Justice 4 Assange, "Inter-American Court of Human Rights, Advisory Opinion OC-25/18" (May 30, 2018), English translation. Copyright © 2018 by Justice 4 Assange. Reprinted by permission. All rights reserved.

Ted Piccone, "How Can International Law Regulate Autonomous Weapons?," Brookings Institution (April 10, 2018). Copyright © 2018 by the Brookings Institution. Reprinted by permission. All rights reserved.

About the Author

Anastasia Telesetsky is a Professor of Law at the University of Idaho College of Law, where she teaches public international law, conflicts of law, international trade and investment law, and international environmental law.

Updates and Commentary in Public International Law, 2019

I. Introduction

This volume covers a selection of international legal developments in 2018 that should be of interest to both students and practitioners of international law. While it is not possible to include all developments, this annual review of public international law highlights some of the major developments that might impact how international law is practiced, including shared expert understandings about customary international law and the interpretation of treaty law in light of subsequent agreements and practice. In some cases, full excerpts or large excerpts from original documents have been provided so that the reader will not have to locate the document. Electronic references are provided.

Some particularly notable developments covered in this volume have received only limited publicity, including the distribution of a draft set of articles on the *Legally Binding Instrument to Regulate in International Human Rights Law the Activities of Transnational Corporations and Other Business Enterprises*. While few generalizations are possible due to the diversity of materials that follow, it is clear that international law as a field continues to evolve in response to contemporary challenges that range from the provision of urban housing to cyberattacks. Hopefully, the materials collected in this volume will inform research and possibly inspire action for practitioners.

II. Sources of Law

The primary sources of public international law are treaties, customary international law (often articulated by international courts), and general principles of law. This volume will highlight several new regional multilateral treaties negotiated and concluded in 2018. This annual will also provide a summary of the International Law Commission's draft conclusions on the meaning of subsequent agreements and practice in international treaty interpretation and on identification of customary international law.

a. Treaties

1. New Multilateral Treaties Negotiated in 2018

Many new multilateral treaties were negotiated in 2018. This section will highlight the adoption of three notable treaties and the negotiation of one additional treaty.

1

In March 2018, eleven Asia-Pacific States under the leadership of Japan representing 13.5% of global gross domestic product adopted the **Comprehensive and Progressive Agreement for Trans-Pacific Partnership** (CPTPP). The United States was originally involved, but it withdrew from the agreement. The new treaty adopted large portions of the previously drafted Trans-Pacific Partnership but also suspended portions of the original text including text regarding intellectual property (e.g., CPTPP allowing for shorter copyright term and pharmaceutical patent protections) and investor-state dispute settlement (e.g., CPTPP did not extended investor-state dispute settlement to the financial sector and limited ability of foreign investors from using investor-state dispute settlement to enforce their contracts with the government).[1] Under the CPTPP, Parties committed to eliminating or reducing tariffs on goods imported from other Parties, as long as the goods qualify as originating under the CPTPP (see Chapter 3). The States agreed that most tariffs will be duty-free upon entry into force of the Agreement, with some tariffs on certain goods gradually eliminated over specific phase-out periods. Parties may not maintain or adopt prohibitions or restrictions on the import or export of any good except under certain situations such as short supply, conservation of natural resources where domestic uses are also restrained, and implementation of domestic price stabilization schemes. In terms of foreign investment, one of the more controversial areas of the agreement, the States agreed that parties are expected to extend fair and nondiscriminatory investment treatment to each other's investors but that governments can still restrict investment activities to achieve legitimate public policy objectives. Two significant chapters of the adopted CPTPP addressed labor and environment in a more comprehensive fashion than most other trade treaties (see Chapters 19 and 20). On December 30, 2018, the CPTPP entered into force for the first six countries to ratify the agreement—Canada, Australia, Japan, Mexico, New Zealand, and Singapore.

In August 2018, the Caspian States of Russia, Kazakhstan, Azerbaijan, Turkmenistan, and Iran signed the **Convention on the Legal Status of the Caspian Sea**. Taking almost 22 years to negotiate, this treaty is notable because it provides a solution to identifying each State's fishing zone within the 371,000 square kilometer sea. On the basis of the treaty, the maritime zones for each State were delineated, and the States agreed to create an exclusive economic zone extending 15 nautical miles from the coastal basepoints plus an additional exclusive fishing zone of 10 nautical

---

1. Comprehensive and Progressive Agreement for Trans-Pacific Partnership (2018) https://international.gc.ca/trade-commerce/trade-agreements-accords-commerciaux/agr-acc/cptpp-ptpgp/text-texte/cptpp-ptpgp.aspx?lang=eng.

miles.[2] For the remaining common area, the States agreed to create a joint fishing management system in which a quota would be divided among all the countries and States could either exchange or sell their portion of the quota with other States.

In October 2018, ten States adopted the **Agreement to Prevent Unregulated High Seas Fisheries in the Central Arctic Ocean**.[3] The treaty is the first legally binding treaty to apply the precautionary approach to protect a 2.8 million square kilometer area from commercial fishing before any extensive commercial fishing has begun. States have agreed not to engage in commercial fishing activities in the high seas portion of the Central Arctic Ocean for an initial period of 16 years with automatic extensions of the moratorium every five years, until one Party objects. Parties will meet every two years to review implementation of the agreement and scientific information gathered as part of a monitoring program.

2018 was also the first year of negotiations at the **Intergovernmental Conference on Marine Biodiversity of Areas Beyond National Jurisdiction**.[4] In September 2018, the Parties discussed capacity building and the transfer of marine technology, area-based management, environmental impact assessments, and marine genetic resources. The conference president was directed to develop a negotiating document that reflected the position of the countries and groups involved that could be used as the basis for continuing negotiations at the second session of the conference in April 2019.

2. Treaty Interpretation in Light of Subsequent Agreements and Subsequent Practice

When disputes arise over treaty interpretation, there have been questions arise about the meaning of Articles 31 and 32 of the Vienna Convention on the Law of the Treaties when providing that interpretation of treaty obligations should take into account subsequent agreements and subsequent practice of the parties as well as more generally subsequent

---

2. Convention on the Legal Status of the Caspian Sea (August 12, 2018) http://en.kremlin.ru/supplement/5328.

3. Agreement to Prevent Unregulated High Seas Fisheries in the Central Arctic Ocean, Annex to Proposal for a Council Decision (2018) https://eur-lex.europa.eu/legal-content/EN/TXT/?uri=COM:2018:453:FIN.

4. International legally binding instrument under the United Nations Convention on the Law of the Sea on the conservation and sustainable use of marine biological diversity of areas beyond national jurisdiction, General Assembly Resolution 72/249 (December 24, 2017) http://undocs.org/en/a/res/72/249.

practice related to the application of a treaty.[5] In 2018, the International Law Commission (ILC) adopted thirteen draft conclusions that are set out below with some excerpts from the commentary as reported to the UN General Assembly.[6]

DRAFT CONCLUSIONS OF SUBSEQUENT AGREEMENTS AND SUBSEQUENT PRACTICE IN RELATION TO THE INTERPRETATION OF TREATIES

CONCLUSION 1   SCOPE

The present draft conclusions concern the role of subsequent agreements and subsequent practice in the interpretation of treaties.

5. Vienna Convention on the Law of Treaties (Vienna, May 23, 1969)

Article 31
General rule of interpretation

1. A treaty shall be interpreted in good faith in accordance with the ordinary meaning to be given to the terms of the treaty in their context and in the light of its object and purpose

2. The context for the purpose of the interpretation of a treaty shall comprise, in addition to the text, including its preamble and annexes:

(a) any agreement relating to the treaty which was made between all the parties in connexion with the conclusion of the treaty; (b) any instrument which was made by one or more parties in connexion with the conclusion of the treaty and accepted by the other parties as an instrument related to the treaty.

3. There shall be taken into account, together with the context:

(a) any subsequent agreement between the parties regarding the interpretation of the treaty or the application of its provisions; (b) any subsequent practice in the application of the treaty which establishes the agreement of the parties regarding its interpretation; (c) any relevant rules of international law applicable in the relations between the parties.

Article 32
Supplementary means of interpretation

Recourse may be had to supplementary means of interpretation, including the preparatory work of the treaty and the circumstances of its conclusion, in order to confirm the meaning resulting from the application of article 31, or to determine the meaning when the interpretation according to article 31:

(a) leaves the meaning ambiguous or obscure; or (b) leads to a result which is manifestly absurd or unreasonable.

6. International Law Commission, Draft Conclusions on Subsequent Agreements and Subsequent Practice in Relation to the Interpretation of Treaties, with Commentaries (2018), A/73/10 para. 52.

CONCLUSION 2   GENERAL RULE AND MEANS OF TREATY INTERPRETATION

1. Articles 31 and 32 of the Vienna Convention on the Law of Treaties set forth, respectively, the general rule of interpretation and the recourse to supplementary means of interpretation. These rules also apply as customary international law.
2. A treaty shall be interpreted in good faith in accordance with the ordinary meaning to be given to its terms in their context and in the light of its object and purpose, as provided in article 31, paragraph 1.
3. Article 31, paragraph 3, provides, *inter alia*, that there shall be taken into account, together with the context, (a) any subsequent agreement between the parties regarding the interpretation of the treaty or the application of its provisions; and (b) any subsequent practice in the application of the treaty which establishes the agreement of the parties regarding its interpretation.
4. Recourse may be had to other subsequent practice in the application of the treaty as a supplementary means of interpretation under article 32.
5. The interpretation of a treaty consists of a single combined operation, which places appropriate emphasis on the various means of interpretation indicated, respectively, in articles 31 and 32.

CONCLUSION 3   SUBSEQUENT AGREEMENTS AND SUBSEQUENT PRACTICE AS AUTHENTIC MEANS OF INTERPRETATION

Subsequent agreements and subsequent practice under article 31, paragraph 3 (a) and (b), being objective evidence of the understanding of the parties as to the meaning of the treaty, are authentic means of interpretation, in the application of the general rule of treaty interpretation reflected in article 31.

CONCLUSION 4   DEFINITION OF SUBSEQUENT AGREEMENT AND SUBSEQUENT PRACTICE

1. A subsequent agreement as an authentic means of interpretation under article 31, paragraph 3 (a), is an agreement between the parties, reached after the conclusion of a treaty, regarding the interpretation of the treaty or the application of its provisions.
2. A subsequent practice as an authentic means of interpretation under article 31, paragraph 3 (b), consists of conduct in the application of a treaty, after its conclusion, which establishes the agreement of the parties regarding the interpretation of the treaty.
3. A subsequent practice as a supplementary means of interpretation under article 32 consists of conduct by one or more parties in the application of the treaty, after its conclusion.

CONCLUSION 5   CONDUCT AS SUBSEQUENT PRACTICE

1. Subsequent practice under articles 31 and 32 may consist of any conduct of a party in the application of a treaty, whether in the exercise of its executive, legislative, judicial, or other functions.
2. Other conduct, including by non-State actors, does not constitute subsequent practice under articles 31 and 32. Such conduct may, however, be relevant when assessing the subsequent practice of parties to a treaty.

Commentary . . . (16) . . . [An] example of conduct of non-State actors that may be relevant when assessing the subsequent practice of States parties is the Landmine and Cluster Munition Monitor, an initiative of the International Campaign to Ban Landmines-Cluster Munitions Coalition. The Monitor acts as a de facto monitoring regime for the 1997 Convention on the Prohibition of the Use, Stockpiling, Production and Transfer of Anti-Personnel Mines and on their Destruction (Ottawa Convention) and the 2008 Convention on Cluster Munitions (Oslo Convention). The Monitor lists pertinent statements and practice by States parties and signatories and identifies, inter alia, interpretative questions concerning the Oslo Convention.

CONCLUSION 6   IDENTIFICATION OF SUBSEQUENT AGREEMENTS AND SUBSEQUENT PRACTICE

1. The identification of subsequent agreements and subsequent practice under article 31, paragraph 3, requires, in particular, a determination whether the parties, by an agreement or a practice, have taken a position regarding the interpretation of the treaty. Such a position is not taken if the parties have merely agreed not to apply the treaty temporarily or agreed to establish a practical arrangement (modus vivendi).
2. Subsequent agreements and subsequent practice under article 31, paragraph 3, may take a variety of forms.
3. The identification of subsequent practice under article 32 requires, in particular, a determination whether conduct by one or more parties is in the application of the treaty.

Commentary . . . (22) . . . The Commission has recognized that subsequent practice under article 31, paragraph 3 (b), consists of any "conduct" in the application of a treaty, including under certain circumstances, inaction, which may contribute to establishing an agreement regarding the interpretation of the treaty. Depending on the treaty concerned, this includes not only externally oriented conduct, such as official acts, statements and voting at the international level, but also internal legislative, executive and judicial acts, and may even include conduct by non-State actors on behalf of one or more States parties and that falls within the scope of what the treaty conceives as forms of its application. Thus, the individual conduct that may contribute to a subsequent practice under article 31, paragraph 3 (b), need not meet any particular formal criteria.

CONCLUSION 7   POSSIBLE EFFECTS OF SUBSEQUENT AGREEMENTS AND SUBSEQUENT PRACTICE IN INTERPRETATION

1. Subsequent agreements and subsequent practice under article 31, paragraph 3, contribute, in their interaction with other means of interpretation, to the clarification of the meaning of a treaty. This may result in narrowing, widening, or otherwise determining the range of possible interpretations, including any scope for the exercise of discretion which the treaty accords to the parties.
2. Subsequent practice under article 32 may also contribute to the clarification of the meaning of a treaty.
3. It is presumed that the parties to a treaty, by an agreement or a practice in the application of the treaty, intend to interpret the treaty, not to amend or to modify it. The possibility of amending or modifying a treaty by subsequent practice of the parties has not been generally recognized. The present draft conclusion is without prejudice to the rules on the amendment or modification of treaties under the 1969 Vienna Convention and under customary international law.

CONCLUSION 8   INTERPRETATION OF TREATY TERMS AS CAPABLE OF EVOLVING OVER TIME

Subsequent agreements and subsequent practice under articles 31 and 32 may assist in determining whether or not the presumed intention of the parties upon the conclusion of the treaty was to give a term used a meaning which is capable of evolving over time.

CONCLUSION 9   WEIGHT OF SUBSEQUENT AGREEMENTS AND SUBSEQUENT PRACTICE AS A MEANS OF INTERPRETATION

1. The weight of a subsequent agreement or subsequent practice as a means of interpretation under article 31, paragraph 3, depends, *inter alia*, on its clarity and specificity.
2. In addition, the weight of subsequent practice under article 31, paragraph 3 (b), depends, *inter alia*, on whether and how it is repeated.

3. The weight of subsequent practice as a supplementary means of interpretation under article 32 may depend on the criteria referred to in paragraphs 1 and 2.

CONCLUSION 10   AGREEMENT OF THE PARTIES REGARDING THE INTERPRETATION OF A TREATY

1. An agreement under article 31, paragraph 3 (a) and (b), requires a common understanding regarding the interpretation of a treaty which the parties are aware of and accept. Such an agreement may, but need not, be legally binding for it to be taken into account.
2. The number of parties that must actively engage in subsequent practice in order to establish an agreement under article 31, paragraph 3 (b), may vary. Silence on the part of one or more parties may constitute acceptance of the subsequent practice when the circumstances call for some reaction.

CONCLUSION 11   DECISIONS ADOPTED WITHIN THE FRAMEWORK OF A CONFERENCE OF STATES PARTIES

1. A Conference of States Parties, under these draft conclusions, is a meeting of parties to a treaty for the purpose of reviewing or implementing the treaty, except where they act as members of an organ of an international organization.
2. The legal effect of a decision adopted within the framework of a Conference of States Parties depends primarily on the treaty and any applicable rules of procedure. Depending on the circumstances, such a decision may embody, explicitly or implicitly, a subsequent agreement under article 31, paragraph 3 (a), or give rise to subsequent practice under article 31, paragraph 3 (b), or to subsequent practice under article 32. Decisions adopted within the framework of a Conference of States Parties often provide a non-exclusive range of practical options for implementing the treaty.
3. A decision adopted within the framework of a Conference of States Parties embodies a subsequent agreement or subsequent practice under article 31, paragraph 3, in so far as it expresses agreement in substance between the parties regarding the interpretation of a treaty, regardless of the form and the procedure by which the decision was adopted, including adoption by consensus.

Commentary . . . (27) Ultimately, the effect of a decision of a Conference of States Parties depends on the circumstances of each particular case and such decisions need to be properly interpreted. A relevant consideration may be whether States parties uniformly or without challenge apply the treaty as interpreted by the Conference of States Parties' decision. Discordant practice following a decision of the Conference of States Parties may be an indication that States did not assume that the decision would be a subsequent agreement under article 31, paragraph 3 (a). Conference of States Parties' decisions that do not qualify as subsequent agreements under article 31, paragraph 3 (a), or as subsequent practice under article 31, paragraph 3 (b), may nevertheless be a subsidiary means of interpretation under article 32.

(32) That certain decisions, despite having been adopted by consensus, cannot represent a subsequent agreement under article 31, paragraph 3(a), is especially true when there exists an objection by one or more States parties to that consensus.

(38) Thus, interpretative resolutions by Conferences of States Parties, even if they are not legally binding as such, can nevertheless be subsequent agreements under article 31, paragraph 3 (a), or subsequent practice under article 31, paragraph 3 (b), if there are sufficient indications that that was the intention of the parties at the time of the adoption of the decision or if the subsequent practice of the parties establishes an agreement on the interpretation of the treaty.

CONCLUSION 12   CONSTITUENT INSTRUMENTS OF INTERNATIONAL ORGANIZATIONS

1. Articles 31 and 32 apply to a treaty which is the constituent instrument of an international organization. Accordingly, subsequent agreements and subsequent practice under article 31, paragraph 3, are, and subsequent practice under article 32 may be, means of interpretation for such treaties.
2. Subsequent agreements and subsequent practice of the parties under article 31, paragraph 3, or subsequent practice under article 32, may arise from, or be expressed in, the practice of an international organization in the application of its constituent instrument.
3. Practice of an international organization in the application of its constituent instrument may contribute to the interpretation of that instrument when applying articles 31 and 32.
4. Paragraphs 1 to 3 apply to the interpretation of any treaty which is the constituent instrument of an international organization without prejudice to any relevant rules of the organization.

CONCLUSION 13   PRONOUNCEMENTS OF EXPERT TREATY BODIES

1. For the purposes of these draft conclusions, an expert treaty body is a body consisting of experts serving in their personal capacity, which is established under a treaty and is not an organ of an international organization.

2. The relevance of a pronouncement of an expert treaty body for the interpretation of a treaty is subject to the applicable rules of the treaty.
3. A pronouncement of an expert treaty body may give rise to, or refer to, a subsequent agreement or subsequent practice by parties under article 31, paragraph 3, or subsequent practice under article 32. Silence by a party shall not be presumed to constitute subsequent practice under article 31, paragraph 3 (b), accepting an interpretation of a treaty as expressed in a pronouncement of an expert treaty body.
4. This draft conclusion is without prejudice to the contribution that pronouncements of expert treaty bodies make to the interpretation of the treaties under their mandates.

Commentary (1) . . . Examples of such expert treaty bodies are the committees established under various human rights treaties at the universal level, for example, the Committee on the Elimination of Racial Discrimination, the Human Rights Committee, the Committee on the Elimination of All Forms of Discrimination against Women, Committee on the Rights of Persons with Disabilities, the Committee on the Rights of the Child and the Committee against Torture. Other expert treaty bodies include the Commission on the Limits of the Continental Shelf under the United Nations Convention on the Law of the Sea, the Compliance Committee under the Convention on Access to Information, Public Participation in Decision-making and Access to Justice in Environmental Matters (Aarhus Convention), and the International Narcotics Control Board under the Single Convention on Narcotic Drugs. . . .

(9) A pronouncement of an expert treaty body cannot as such constitute a subsequent agreement or subsequent practice under article 31, paragraph 3 (a) or (b), since this provision requires an agreement of the parties or subsequent practice of the parties that establishes their agreement regarding the interpretation of the treaty. . . .

(11) Pronouncements of expert treaty bodies may, however, give rise to, or refer to, a subsequent agreement or a subsequent practice by the parties which establish their agreement regarding the interpretation of the treaty under article 31, paragraph 3 (a) or (b). . . . There is indeed no reason why a subsequent agreement between the parties or subsequent practice that establishes the agreement of the parties themselves regarding the interpretation of a treaty could not arise from, or be referred to by, a pronouncement of an expert treaty body. . . .

(13) One possible way of identifying an agreement of the parties regarding the interpretation of a treaty that is reflected in a pronouncement of an expert treaty body is to look at resolutions of organs of international organizations as well as of Conferences of States Parties. General Assembly resolutions may, in particular, explicitly or implicitly refer to pronouncements of expert treaty bodies . . . [finding that a resolution adopted without votes may constitute subsequent agreement of parties].

b. Identification of Customary International Law

In 2018, the International Law Commission (ILC) provided its draft conclusions to assist international lawyers, States, and national courts with determining the existence and the content of customary international rules. The content and parameters of customary international law are difficult to determine because they are unwritten. The ILC's work is particularly significant in assisting practitioners with determining what evidence might be important for finding the formation of customary international law. The ILC began work in this area in 2012. The most recent report on the topic built on research collected by the Secretariat from States about what they regard as adequate evidence of customary international law.[7] In 2018, the ILC adopted the following sixteen draft conclusions with commentary to be submitted to the UN General Assembly.[8]

DRAFT CONCLUSIONS ON IDENTIFICATION OF CUSTOMARY INTERNATIONAL LAW WITH COMMENTARIES

CONCLUSION 1 SCOPE

The present draft conclusions concern the way in which the existence and content of rules of customary international law are to be determined.

CONCLUSION 2   TWO CONSTITUENT ELEMENTS

To determine the existence and content of a rule of customary international law, it is necessary to ascertain whether there is a general practice that is accepted as law (*opinio juris*).

Commentary: (1) . . . [T]he identification of a rule of customary international law requires an inquiry into two distinct, yet related, questions: whether there is a general practice, and whether such general practice is accepted as law (that is, accompanied by *opinio juris*). In other words, one must look at what States actually do and seek to determine whether they recognize an obligation or a right to act in that way. This methodology, the "two-element approach", underlies the draft conclusions and is widely supported by States, in case law, and in scholarly writings. It serves to ensure

---

7. UN General Assembly, International Law Commission, 70th Session, Identification of Customary International Law, Ways and Means for Making the Evidence of Customary International Law More Readily Available, Memorandum by the Secretariat A/CN.4/710 (January 12, 2018).

8. International Law Commission, Draft Conclusions on Identification of Customary International Law, with Commentaries A/73/10 (2018) para. 66.

that the exercise of identifying rules of customary international law results in determining only such rules as actually exist. . . .

(4) [T]he presence of only one constituent element does not suffice for the identification of a rule of customary international law. Practice without acceptance as law (*opinio juris*), even if widespread and consistent, can be no more than a non-binding usage, while a belief that something is (or ought to be) the law unsupported by practice is mere aspiration; it is the two together that establish the existence of a rule of customary international law. . . .

CONCLUSION 3   ASSESSMENT OF EVIDENCE FOR THE TWO CONSTITUENT ELEMENTS

1. In assessing evidence for the purpose of ascertaining whether there is a general practice and whether that practice is accepted as law (*opinio juris*), regard must be had to the overall context, the nature of the rule and the particular circumstances in which the evidence in question is to be found.

2. Each of the two constituent elements is to be separately ascertained. This requires an assessment of evidence for each element.

Commentary . . . (4) . . . In particular, where prohibitive rules are concerned, it may sometimes be difficult to find much affirmative State practice (as opposed to inaction); cases involving such rules are more likely to turn on evaluating whether the inaction is accepted as law.

CONCLUSION 4   REQUIREMENT OF PRACTICE

1. The requirement of a general practice, as a constituent element of customary international law, refers primarily to the practice of States that contributes to the formation, or expression, of rules of customary international law.

2. In certain cases, the practice of international organizations also contributes to the formation, or expression, of rules of customary international law.

3. Conduct of other actors is not practice that contributes to the formation, or expression, of rules of customary international law, but may be relevant when assessing the practice referred to in paragraphs 1 and 2.

Commentary . . . (8) Paragraph 3 makes explicit that the conduct of entities other than States and international organizations—for example, non-governmental organizations (NGOs) and private individuals, but also transnational corporations and non-State armed groups—is neither creative nor expressive of customary international law. As such, their conduct does not contribute to the formation, or expression, of rules of customary international law, and may not serve as direct (primary) evidence of the existence and content of such rules. The paragraph recognizes, however, that such conduct may have an indirect role in the identification of customary international law, by stimulating or recording the practice and acceptance as law (*opinio juris*) of States and international organizations. For example, the acts of private individuals may sometimes be relevant to the formation or expression of rules of customary international law, but only to the extent that States have endorsed or reacted to them.

(9) Official statements of the International Committee of the Red Cross (ICRC), such as appeals for and memorandums on respect for international humanitarian law, may likewise play an important role in shaping the practice of States reacting to such statements; and publications of the ICRC may assist in identifying relevant practice. Such activities may thus contribute to the development and determination of customary international law, but they are not practice as such.

CONCLUSION 5   CONDUCT OF THE STATE AS STATE PRACTICE

State practice consists of conduct of the State, whether in the exercise of its executive, legislative, judicial or other functions.

CONCLUSION 6   FORMS OF PRACTICE

1. Practice may take a wide range of forms. It includes both physical and verbal acts. It may, under certain circumstances, include inaction.

2. Forms of State practice include, but are not limited to: diplomatic acts and correspondence; conduct in connection with resolutions adopted by an international organization or at an intergovernmental conference; conduct in connection with treaties; executive conduct, including operational conduct "on the ground"; legislative and administrative acts; and decisions of national courts.

3. There is no predetermined hierarchy among the various forms of practice.

CONCLUSION 7   ASSESSING A STATE'S PRACTICE

1. Account is to be taken of all available practice of a particular State, which is to be assessed as a whole.

2. Where the practice of a particular State varies, the weight to be given to that practice may, depending on the circumstances, be reduced.

CONCLUSION 8   THE PRACTICE MUST BE GENERAL

1. The relevant practice must be general, meaning that it must be sufficiently widespread and representative, as well as consistent.

2. Provided that the practice is general, no particular duration is required.

CONCLUSION 9   REQUIREMENT OF ACCEPTANCE AS LAW (*OPINIO JURIS*)

1. The requirement, as a constituent element of customary international law, that the general practice be accepted as law (*opinio juris*) means that the practice in question must be undertaken with a sense of legal right or obligation.

2. A general practice that is accepted as law (*opinio juris*) is to be distinguished from mere usage or habit.

CONCLUSION 10   FORMS OF EVIDENCE OF ACCEPTANCE
AS LAW (*OPINIO JURIS*)

1. Evidence of acceptance as law (*opinio juris*) may take a wide range of forms.

2. Forms of evidence of acceptance as law (*opinio juris*) include, but are not limited to: public statements made on behalf of States; official publications; government legal opinions; diplomatic correspondence; decisions of national courts; treaty provisions; and conduct in connection with resolutions adopted by an international organization or at an intergovernmental conference.

3. Failure to react over time to a practice may serve as evidence of acceptance as law (*opinio juris*), provided that States were in a position to react and the circumstances called for some reaction.

CONCLUSION 11   TREATIES

1. A rule set forth in a treaty may reflect a rule of customary international law if it is established that the treaty rule:

    (a) codified a rule of customary international law existing at the time when the treaty was concluded;

    (b) has led to the crystallization of a rule of customary international law that had started to emerge prior to the conclusion of the treaty; or

    (c) has given rise to a general practice that is accepted as law (*opinio juris*), thus generating a new rule of customary international law.

2. The fact that a rule is set forth in a number of treaties may, but does not necessarily, indicate that the treaty rule reflects a rule of customary international law.

Commentary . . . (3) The number of parties to a treaty may be an important factor in determining whether particular rules set forth therein reflect customary international law; treaties that have obtained near-universal acceptance may be seen as particularly indicative in this respect . . . . The attitude of States not party to a widely ratified treaty, both at the time of its conclusion and subsequently, will also be of relevance.

CONCLUSION 12   RESOLUTIONS OF INTERNATIONAL ORGANIZATIONS AND INTERGOVERNMENTAL CONFERENCES

1. A resolution adopted by an international organization or at an intergovernmental conference cannot, of itself, create a rule of customary international law.

2. A resolution adopted by an international organization or at an intergovernmental conference may provide evidence for determining the existence and content of a rule of customary international law, or contribute to its development.

3. A provision in a resolution adopted by an international organization or at an intergovernmental conference may reflect a rule of customary international law if it is established that the provision corresponds to a general practice that is accepted as law (*opinio juris*).

CONCLUSION 13   DECISIONS OF COURTS AND TRIBUNALS

1. Decisions of international courts and tribunals, in particular of the International Court of Justice, concerning the existence and content of rules of customary international law are a subsidiary means for the determination of such rules.

2. Regard may be had, as appropriate, to decisions of national courts concerning the existence and content of rules of customary international law, as a subsidiary means for the determination of such rules.

CONCLUSION 14   TEACHINGS

Teachings of the most highly qualified publicists of the various nations may serve as a subsidiary means for the determination of rules of customary international law.

CONCLUSION 15 PERSISTENT OBJECTOR

1. Where a State has objected to a rule of customary international law while that rule was in the process of formation, the rule is not opposable to the State concerned for so long as it maintains its objection.

2. The objection must be clearly expressed, made known to other States, and maintained persistently.

3. The present draft conclusion is without prejudice to any question concerning peremptory norms of general international law (*jus cogens*).

Commentary . . . (5) . . . The timeliness of the objection is critical: the State must express its opposition before a given practice has crystallized into a rule of customary international law, and its position will be best assured if it did so at the earliest possible moment. While the line between objection and violation may not always be an easy one to draw, there is no such thing as a subsequent objector rule: once the rule has come into being, an objection will not avail a State wishing to exempt itself.

CONCLUSION 16 PARTICULAR CUSTOMARY INTERNATIONAL LAW

1. A rule of particular customary international law, whether regional, local or other, is a rule of customary international law that applies only among a limited number of States.

2. To determine the existence and content of a rule of particular customary international law, it is necessary to ascertain whether there is a general practice among the States concerned that is accepted by them as law (*opinio juris*) among themselves.

III. States

Today the United Nations has 193 members. The Holy See and Palestine are non-member States that participate as observers. This section provides summaries of developments regarding the status of Western Sahara and Palestine.

a. Western Sahara

The United Nations has continued negotiations in the disputed Western Sahara Area. Security Council Resolution 2440, approved in October 2018, reauthorized a six-month extension for the United Nations Mission for a Referendum in Western Sahara. The Russian Federation, Bolivia, and Ethiopia abstained on this vote. The governments of Morocco, Algeria, and Mauritania as well as the Popular Front for the Liberation of Saguía-el-Hamra and Río de Oro are seeking a political solution to provide for the self-determination of the people of Western Sahara. These developments are in keeping with the International Court of Justice's 1975 advisory opinion recognizing the principle of self-determination for the people of Western Sahara.[9]

b. Palestine

In September 2018, the State of Palestine filed a complaint against the United States when the U.S. government moved its embassy from Tel Aviv, Israel to the city of Jerusalem in violation of the 1961 Vienna Convention of Diplomatic Relations requiring a State to locate an embassy on the territory of the host State.[10] The jurisdictional basis of the suit is Article 1 of the Optional Protocol to the Vienna Convention, requiring compulsory settlement of disputes. Palestine acceded to the Vienna Convention on April 2, 2014, and to the Optional Protocol on March 22, 2018. The United States has been a party to both the Convention and the Protocol since November 13, 1972. Palestine deposited on July 4, 2018, a "Declaration Recognizing the Competence of the International Court of Justice," which stated that Palestine "accept[ed] with immediate effect the competence of the International Court of Justice for the settlement of all disputes that may arise or that have already arisen by Article I of the Optional Protocol to the Vienna Convention." The United States has informed the International Court of Justice that it is not in a "treaty relationship" with Palestine under the Vienna Convention or the Optional Protocol because the United States does not recognize Palestine as a State. The United States has not appointed an agent for the case. The International Court of Justice has requested memorials and counter-memorials from the parties on the jurisdiction of the court and the admissibility of the application to be filed in 2019. The United States shut down the Palestinian Liberation

9. Western Sahara, Advisory Opinion, I.C.J. Reports 1975, p. 12 (para 162) ("[T]he Court's conclusion is that the materials and information presented to it do not establish any tie of territorial sovereignty between the territory of Western Sahara and the Kingdom of Morocco or the Mauritanian entity. Thus, the Court has not found legal ties of such a nature as might affect the application of resolution 1514 (XV) in the decolonization of Western Sahara and, in particular, of the principle of self-determination through the free and genuine expression of the will of the peoples of the Territory.").

10. Relocation of the United States Embassy to Jerusalem (Palestine v. United States of America) (2018), Application of Proceedings to the International Court of Justice.

Organization mission in Washington, D.C. because of its alleged refusal to cooperate with the U.S. government on peace efforts and its support of an International Criminal Court investigation of Israel. The United States has also withheld its contributions from the United Nations Relief and Works Agency for Palestine Refugees.

Palestine has continued to play an active role in international organizations. By a recorded vote of 146 in favor to 3 against (Australia, Israel, United States), with 15 abstentions, the UN General Assembly decided to grant the State of Palestine the right to make statements, introduce proposals and amendments, and raise procedural motions.[11]

IV. International Organizations

While there is a proliferation of international organizations, especially international agencies that have their own legal developments, this section will only focus on major resolutions adopted by the UN General Assembly (UNGA) and the UN Security Council. General Assembly resolutions are not binding but can contribute to the formation of customary international law. Security Council resolutions are binding.

a. UN General Assembly

The UNGA adopted a number of political resolutions calling upon specific States to refrain from certain ongoing political actions. For example, the UNGA adopted a resolution proposed by Ukraine calling for an end to the militarization of Crimea by a vote of 66 in favor, 19 opposed, and 72 abstentions.[12] The resolution called on the Russian Federation to stop impeding the lawful exercise of navigational rights and freedoms by neighboring States and emphasized that the presence of Russian troops in Crimea is contrary to the territorial integrity of Ukraine. By a vote of 189 in favor and 2 against, the UNGA adopted its annual resolution calling for the United States to ends its commercial and financial embargo of Cuba.

A partial list of notable resolutions that display the wide variety of topics debated by the Assembly in 2018 include:

- Impact of rapid technological change on the achievement of the Sustainable Development Goals and targets, A/RES/73/17

---

11. UN General Assembly, Group of 77, A/73/L.5 (October 10, 2018).

12. Problem of the Militarization of the Autonomous Republic of Crimea and the City of Sevastopol, Ukraine, as well as Parts of the Black and Azov, A/73/L.47 (December 17, 2018) https://digitallibrary.un.org/record/1654630/files/A_73_L-47-EN.pdf.

- Peaceful Settlement of the Question of Palestine, A/RES/73/19
- African Nuclear-Weapon-Free Zone Treaty, A/RES/73/26
- No First Placement of Weapons in Outer Space, A/RES/73/31
- Relationship between disarmament and development, A/RES/73/37
- Convention on the Prohibition of the Use of Nuclear Weapons, A/RES/73/74
- Oceans and the Law of the Sea, A/RES/73/124
- Enlightenment and Religious Tolerance, A/RES/73/128
- Return or restitution of cultural property to the countries of origin, A/RES/73/130
- Scope, modalities, format and organization of the high-level meeting on universal health coverage, A/RES/73/131
- Protecting children from bullying, A/RES/73/154
- Use of mercenaries as a means of violating human rights and impeding the exercise of the right of peoples to self-determination, A/RES/73/158
- Universal Realization of the right of peoples to self-determination, A/RES/73/160
- United Nations Declaration on the Rights of Peasants and Other People Working in Rural Areas, A/RES/73/165
- The rule of law in crime prevention and criminal justice in the context of Sustainable Development, A/RES/73/185
- Global Compact for Safe, Orderly and Regular Migration, A/RES/73/194
- Subsequent Agreements and Subsequent Practice in Relation to the Interpretation of Treaties, A/RES/73/202 [See Part II.a.2.]
- Identification of customary law, A/RES/73/203 [See Part II.b.]
- The Rule of Law at the National and International Levels, A/RES/73/207
- The Scope and Application of the Principle of Universal Jurisdiction, A/RES/73/208
- Strengthening and Promoting the International Treaty Framework, A/RES/73/210
- Permanent Sovereignty of the Palestinian people in the Occupied Palestinian Territory, including East Jerusalem and of the Arab Population in the occupied Syrian Golan over their Natural Resources, A/73/255

b.   Security Council

In 2018, the Security Council continued to respond to political instability with a number of resolutions adopted regarding the Middle East, Central African Republic, Somalia, Bosnia and Herzegovina, Libya, Western Sahara, Mali, Cyprus, Iraq, Guinea-Bissau, Afghanistan, Burundi, Haiti, and Democratic Republic of the Congo. Resolutions adopted in 2018 are available at http://research.un.org/en/docs/sc/quick/meetings/2018.

Three general resolutions are notable. On May 24, the Security Council unanimously adopted resolution 2417 on the protection of civilians during armed conflict. Focused on the withholding of food as a tool of violence, the resolution unequivocally called upon States to exercise their State responsibilities to protect civilians. Specifically, States are called upon to take "constant care to spare civilian objects, including objects necessary for food production and distribution such as farms, markets, water systems, mills, food processing and storage sites, and hubs and means for food transportation, and [to] refrain . . . from attacking, destroying, removing or rendering useless objects that are indispensable to the survival of the civilian population, such as foodstuffs, crops, livestock, agricultural assets, drinking water installations and supplies, and irrigation works, and respecting and protecting humanitarian personnel and consignments used for humanitarian relief operation."[13]

On July 9, the Security Council unanimously adopted resolution 2427 calling for States to address the use of children in armed conflict. The Security Council specifically condemns "the recruitment and use of children by parties to armed conflict as well as their re-recruitment, killing and maiming, rape and other forms of sexual violence, abductions, attacks against schools and hospitals as well as denial of humanitarian access by parties to armed conflict and all other violations of international law, including international humanitarian law, human rights law and refugee law, committed against children in situations of armed conflict and demands that all relevant parties immediately put an end to such practices and take special measures to protect children."[14]

On September 21, the Security Council unanimously adopted resolution 2436 reaffirming support for reforming peacekeeping missions to ensure clear objective standards for measuring performance of peace keeping personnel. The Council reiterated that host countries must protect civilians and affirmed "the need for peacekeeping missions with a mandate that includes the protection of civilians to ensure full mandate implementation, and underlines that where mandated, peacekeepers are authorized to use all necessary means, which includes the use of force when required, in order to protect civilians under threat of physical violence."[15]

V. *International Disputes*

While it is not possible to summarize all of the notable decisions by international courts, tribunals, and committees, this section will provide a short selection of key international decisions from 2018.

---

13. Resolution 2417, S/RES/2417 (May 24, 2018).
14. Resolution 2427, S/RES/2427 (July 9, 2018).
15. Resolution 2436, S/RES/2436 (September 21, 2018).

a. International Court of Justice

The International Court of Justice (ICJ) delivered judgments in a variety of disputes in 2018. In February 2018, the ICJ decided in *Certain Activities Carried Out by Nicaragua in the Border Area (Costa Rica v. Nicaragua)* the amount of compensation that Nicaragua should pay Costa Rica for having caused damage to Costa Rican territory by dredging and constructing a canal.[16] The basis of the court's decision was the legal principle requiring a State to make full reparation for damage caused by a wrongful act. This judgment was the first time that the Court had adjudicated a claim for environmental damages to cover reparations associated with damages to a wetland. The court decided that full reparation would include (1) indemnification for the impairment or loss of environmental goods and services and (2) payment for active restoration. Costa Rica argued for an "ecosystem services" approach to compensation while Nicaragua argued for "replacement costs approach." The court chose not to use exclusively either approach but instead found that Nicaragua had impacted four categories of environmental goods and services (trees, other raw materials, air quality services, biodiversity) and was responsible for U.S. $120,000 to cover impairment/loss of environmental goods and services and U.S. $2,708 for restoration. The ICJ assigned additional compensation to Costa Rica for costs and expenses.

Also in February 2018, the Court delivered its decision in *Maritime Delimitation in the Caribbean Sea and the Pacific Ocean (Costa Rica v. Nicaragua)*.[17] In this decision, the court assigned a territorial sea maritime boundary between the two countries using a delimitation methodology that it has used in previous cases: the Court drew a provisional median line and then considered whether any existing special circumstances would justify adjusting the line. The Court found a special circumstance due to a sandspit between the two States. The sandspit had become a subject of dispute between the States as Nicaragua had established a military camp there that had violated Costa Rica's sovereignty. A maritime boundary was also assigned for the exclusive economic zone and the continental shelf on the basis of (1) drawing a provisional equidistant line using basepoints on the relevant coasts of the parties, (2) determining whether relevant circumstances require an adjustment of the line, and (3) assessing the equitableness of the line by checking whether there exists "a marked disproportionality" between the length of the Parties' coasts and the maritime

---

16. Certain Activities Carried Out by Nicaragua in the Border Area (Costa Rica v. Nicaragua), International Court of Justice, Compensation Owed by the Republic of Nicaragua to the Republic of Costa Rica (February 2, 2018).

17. Maritime Delimitation in the Caribbean Sea and the Pacific Ocean (Costa Rica v. Nicaragua), International Court of Justice, Judgment on the Merits (February 2, 2018).

areas assigned to them. The Court did make some adjustments of the line on the basis of small features but did not find any disproportionality between Costa Rica's and Nicaragua's maritime areas.

In July 2019, the ICJ issued provisional measures in *Application of the International Convention on the Elimination of All Forms of Racial Discrimination (Qatar v. United Arab Emirates)*.[18] Qatar brought the case after the United Arab Emirates allegedly expelled on June 5, 2017, Qataris from the UAE on the basis of their national origin in violation of specific human rights including right to marriage, right to choice of spouse, right to public health, right to education, right to own property, right to work, and right to equal treatment before tribunals. The Court found that it is plausible on the basis of existing evidence that there may have been acts of racial discrimination. In a close vote of 8 to 7, the Court decided that the UAE must ensure that families that include a Qatari who was expelled on June 5, 2017 must be reunited, impacted Qatari students must have the opportunity to complete their education or obtain educational records, and Qataris must be given access to tribunals in the UAE.

On October 1, 2018, the ICJ issued its final decision in *Obligation to Negotiate Access to the Pacific Ocean (Bolivia v. Chile)*.[19] This case was brought by Bolivia who requested that the ICJ order Chile to negotiate with landlocked Bolivia to provide coastal access to the ocean. Bolivia argued that Chile had entered into a number of bilateral agreements with Bolivia that indicated that Chile would negotiate some form of access. Ultimately, the Court held that none of the instruments were specific enough to establish a legal obligation to negotiate. Likewise, the Court found that any unilateral declaration of Chile to assist Bolivia to overcome "the obstacles that limit Bolivia's development on account of its landlocked condition" was not a legal commitment. Bolivia's arguments based on estoppel and acquiescence similarly failed to persuade the Court. The Court also explored a novel claim that Chile had frustrated Bolivia's "legitimate expectations" but ultimately found that there was no international legal principle based on legitimate expectations. Finally, the Court examined the UN Charter, Charter of the Organization of American States (OAS), and General Assembly resolutions and decided that none of them created legal obligations for Chile. The Court found that Chile had not breached any legal obligation toward Bolivia but hoped that the two States would continue to maintain productive dialogue.

Finally, on October 3, 2018, the ICJ issued an order in support of provisional measures in the case *Alleged Violations of the 1955 Treaty of Amity, Economic Relations, and Consular Rights (Islamic Republic of Iran v. United*

---

18. Application of the International Convention on the Elimination of All Forms of Racial Discrimination (Qatar v. United Arab Emirates), International Court of Justice, Request for the Indication of Provisional Measures (July 23, 2018).

19. Obligation to Negotiate Access to the Pacific Ocean (Bolivia v. Chile), International Court of Justice, Judgment on the Merits (October 1, 2018).

States). This case arose when the U.S. President issued a memorandum ending the participation of the United States in the Joint Comprehensive Plan of Action (an agreement reached by Iran, the EU, Germany, and the five permanent members of the UN Security Council) and reinstating sanctions. Iran seeks to challenge the imposition of the sanctions under the 1955 Treaty designed to prohibit restrictions on the import and export of products originating from the two countries. The Court found that restrictions placed by the United States on goods required for humanitarian needs and safety of civil aviation might violate the terms of the 1955 treaty and have detrimental impacts on the health and lives of individuals living in the territory of Iran. The Court ordered the United States to remove impediments to trade in medicines and medical devices; foodstuffs and agricultural commodities; and spare parts and equipment necessary for the safety of civil aviation.[20] On October 3, 2018, the United States gave its one-year notice that it would be terminating the 1955 Treaty with Iran.

b.   International Criminal Court

In 2018, while the International Criminal Court (ICC) continued to attract scrutiny from State Representatives from both parties and nonparties to the ICC, the Court issued a number of significant rulings and continued to collect information for a number of investigations. In February, the ICC prosecutor announced a preliminary examination to determine whether crimes under the Rome Statute have been taking place in Venezuela since 2017. Later in September, member States of the ICC asked the ICC to investigate potential crimes in Venezuela since 2014. Also in February, the ICC began a preliminary examination of possible crimes against humanity by Filipino leader Rodrigo Duterte, who responded by terminating the membership of the Philippines in the ICC.[21]

In June 2018, the Appeals Chamber of the ICC acquitted Jean-Pierre Bemba Gombo of the charges of war crimes and crimes against humanity.[22] The majority reversed the 2016 Trial Chamber decision that found that Mr. Bemba was not criminally responsible for the crimes against humanity of murder and rape and the war crimes of murder, rape, and pillaging

---

20. Alleged Violations of the 1955 Treaty of Amity, Economic Relations, and Consular Rights (Islamic Republic of Iran v. United States), International Court of Justice, Request for the Indication of Provisional Measures, Order (October 3, 2018).

21. Philippines informs U.N. of ICC withdrawal, court regrets move (March 16, 2018) https://www.reuters.com/article/us-philippines-duterte-icc-un/philippines-informs-u-n-of-icc-withdrawal-court-regrets-move-idUSKCN1GS0Y5.

22. International Criminal Court, Judgment on the Appeal of Mr. Jean-Pierre Bemba Gombo against Trial Chamber III's 'Judgment pursuant to Article 74 of the Statute' (June 8, 2018).

committed by the *Mouvement de liberation du Congo* troops in the Central African Republic.

Also in June 2018, a pretrial chamber was formed to decide whether the ICC has jurisdiction over Palestinian claims of war crimes related to the 2014 Gaza war and the construction of settlements in the West Bank by Israel. On July 13, 2018, the pretrial chamber judges requested victims of the situation in Palestine to submit relevant information to the court. The Israeli government formally protested the judges' actions. In September 2018, Palestine filed an additional claim with the ICC seeking a declaration that Israel's plan to raze a West Bank Bedouin village would constitute a war crime.

In July 2018, the Trial Chamber II of the ICC decided that reparations were not available for transgenerational harm. In the case *The Prosecutor v. Germain Katanga*, five applicants for reparations claimed that they should be entitled to compensation for psychological harms caused when social violence and trauma (such as post-traumatic stress disorder) are transmitted from parents to children through some combination of epigenetics and social upbringing.[23] Taking each case individually, the court found that the applicants had not established a causal link between psychological harms and the crimes of the defendant.

In July 2018, the amendment to the Rome Statute to add the crime of aggression came into effect with the ratification of 35 member States.[24] The law is not retrospective, but politicians and military leaders can now be held individually responsible for invasion even when a war has not been declared. From July 2018 onwards, the ICC will be able to seek prosecutions under Article 8bis(3) for the following actions:

(a) The invasion or attack by the armed forces of a State of the territory of another State, or any military occupation, however temporary, resulting from such invasion or attack, or any annexation by the use of force of the territory of another State or part thereof;

(b) Bombardment by the armed forces of a State against the territory of another State or the use of any weapons by a State against the territory of another State;

(c) The blockade of the ports or coasts of a State by the armed forces of another State;

---

23. International Criminal Court, Situation in The Democratic Republic of the Congo in the Case of the Prosecutor v. Germain Katanga, Decision on the Matter of the Transgenerational Harm Alleged by Some Applicants for Reparations Remanded by the Appeals Chamber in its Judgment of 8 March 2018, (July 19, 2018) https://www.icc-cpi.int/CourtRecords/CR2018_04641.PDF.

24. Rome Statute, Article 8bis, https://www.icc-cpi.int/NR/rdonlyres/ADD16852-AEE9-4757-ABE7-9CDC7CF02886/283503/RomeStatutEngl.pdf.

(d) An attack by the armed forces of a State on the land, sea or air forces, or marine and air fleets of another State;

(e) The use of armed forces of one State which are within the territory of another State with the agreement of the receiving State, in contravention of the conditions provided for in the agreement or any extension of their presence in such territory beyond the termination of the agreement;

(f) The action of a State in allowing its territory, which it has placed at the disposal of another State, to be used by that other State for perpetrating an act of aggression against a third State;

(g) The sending by or on behalf of a State of armed bands, groups, irregulars or mercenaries, which carry out acts of armed force against another State of such gravity as to amount to the acts listed above, or its substantial involvement therein.

In September 2018, the Pre-Trial Chamber I of the ICC decided that the Court had the authority to exercise jurisdiction over the alleged expulsion of the Rohingya people from Myanmar to Bangladesh.[25] The Rohingya are a majority Muslim ethnic group who have historically lived in Rakhine State in Myanmar and have been persecuted by Myanmar's military for decades. The Myanmar security forces are alleged to have attacked Rohingya villages leading to a situation in which over 400,000 people have fled to Bangladesh. Even though Myanmar is not a party to the Rome Statute, the Court found that it has jurisdiction because one element of the crime against humanity of forced deportation (e.g., the crossing of the border) took place on Bangladeshi territory. Bangladesh is a party to the Rome Statute.

Also in September, the ICC prosecutor asked the Court's Pre-trial Chamber to open a formal investigation into the possible commission of war crimes and crimes against humanity committed by parties to the war in Afghanistan after receiving 1.7 million allegations of war crimes during a three-month period. In response to this announcement, the U.S. national security adviser threatened interference with ICC financing and with the operation of the institution if any U.S. nationals or nationals from U.S. allies might be prosecuted for war crimes.

In November 2018, Russian mercenaries and military veterans asked the ICC to prosecute Russia's private military companies for war crimes in relation to secret deployments to Syria, Ukraine, and Africa.[26]

---

25. International Criminal Court, Decision on the 'Prosecution's Request for a Ruling on Jurisdiction under Article 19(3) of the Statute' (September 6, 2018).

26. Russian military veterans seek ICC investigation of mercenary deployments (November 9, 2018) https://www.reuters.com/article/us-russia-military-mercenaries/russian-military-veterans-seek-icc-investigation-of-mercenary-deployments-idUSKCN1NE2G7.

c. Inter-American Court of Human Rights

In May 2018, the Inter-American Court of Human Rights, a regional court designed to enforce the American Convention on Human Rights, issued a significant advisory opinion on the right to seek asylum. The opinion was provided in response to Ecuador's 2016 questions regarding what human rights law applies to diplomatic asylum particularly in the case of Julian Assange, the high-profile founder of Wikileaks who has been living in the Ecuador embassy in London for six years.[27] The following questions were posed:

> A) Taking into account, in particular, the principles of equality and non-discrimination based on any social condition established in Articles 2(1), 5 and 26 of the International Covenant on Civil and Political Rights, the *pro homine* principle, and the obligation to respect all human rights of every person in every circumstance and without adverse distinctions, as well as Articles 31 and 32 of the 1969 Vienna Convention on the Law of Treaties, Article 29 of the American Convention on Human Rights, and Articles 28 and 30 of the Universal Declaration of Human Rights: Is it admissible that a State, group, or individual execute actions or adopt a conduct that, in practice, signifies disregard for the provisions established in the human rights instruments mentioned above, including Article 5 of the Geneva Convention relating to the Status of Refugees and thus attributes to Articles 22(7) and XXVII of the American Convention and of the American Declaration of the Rights and Duties of Man, respectively, a restricted content as regards the form or method of asylum, and what should be the legal consequences on human rights and fundamental freedoms of persons affected by such a regressive interpretation?

> B) Is it admissible that a State, which is not a party to a specific convention on asylum, obstructs, prevents or restricts the action of another State that is a party to that convention, so that the latter is unable to fulfill the obligations and commitments it assumed under that instrument, and what should be the legal consequences of this conduct for the person who has been granted asylum?

> C) Is it admissible that a State, which is not a party to a specific convention on asylum, or which belongs to a different regional legal system from the one based on which asylum was granted, hand over the person who has been granted asylum or refugee status to the agent of persecution, violating the principle of non-refoulement, on the pretext that the person granted asylum loses this condition because he is in a country outside the said legal system due to exercising his right to freedom of movement, and what should be the legal consequences of this conduct on the right of asylum and the human rights of the person granted asylum? [Additional questions followed.]

27. Inter-American Court of Human Rights, Request for an Advisory Opinion (2018) http://www.corteidh.or.cr/docs/solicitudoc/solicitud_18_08_16_eng.pdf.

In a lengthy decision, the court responded to Ecuador's questions. Excerpts from the Court's response are provided here:[28]

[In response to Question A] 155. As mentioned above, there is no universal agreement under public international law on the existence of an individual right to receive diplomatic asylum, although this could be an effective mechanism to protect individuals from circumstances that make democratic life difficult in a given country. This lack of international consensus does not imply that recourse to diplomatic asylum should be ruled out, since States retain the sovereign power to grant it. Indeed, individuals have sought asylum in diplomatic missions for centuries, and States, in turn, have granted some form of protection to individuals persecuted for political reasons or facing an imminent threat to their life, liberty, security and/or integrity, not always recognizing diplomatic asylum, but often resorting to diplomatic negotiations. To this extent, in accordance with international law, diplomatic asylum consists of a humanitarian practice for the purpose of protecting fundamental human rights, which has been granted for the purpose of saving lives or preventing damage to rights in the face of an imminent threat.

156. In conclusion, the Court interprets that diplomatic asylum is not protected under Article 22(7) of the American Convention or Article XXVII of the American Declaration. In short, the right to seek and receive asylum within the framework of the inter-American system is configured as a human right to seek and receive international protection in a foreign territory, including with this expression refugee status according to the pertinent United Nations instruments or relevant national legislation, and territorial asylum in accordance with the various inter-American conventions on the subject. . . .

158. Finally, the Court considers it pertinent to rule on the argument that diplomatic asylum would be a regional custom. The Court notes that, in order to determine the existence of a rule of customary international law, it is necessary to verify: (i) a general practice of States, and (ii) their acceptance as law (*opinio juris sive necessitatis*), that is, that they must be followed with the conviction of the existence of a legal obligation or right.

158. In this case, a customary rule of a regional nature is alleged, which is particular and not universal in scope. The International Court of Justice, in the aforementioned Asylum Case (*Colombia v. Peru*), determined that a regional customary rule could be established as long as the existence of uniform and consistent use as an expression of a right of the State granting asylum is proved. However, in view of the broad nature of its advisory jurisdiction, the Inter-American Court considers that it is appropriate to assess that character within the framework of the 35 Member States of the OAS, in the general

---

28. Inter-American Court of Human Rights, Advisory Opinion OC-25/18 (May 30, 2018) http://www.corteidh.or.cr/docs/opiniones/seriea_25_esp.pdf; Spanish original translated at https://justice4assange.com/IMG/pdf/Inter-American_Court_Advisory_Opinion_OC-25-18-2.pdf.

interest and without limiting the scope of its advisory opinions to only a few States.

159. However, the Court notes that not all OAS Member States are parties to the various conventions on diplomatic asylum and, furthermore, as already stated, these conventions are not uniform in their terminology or provisions, since they respond to a progressive development of the regulation of diplomatic asylum in response to certain situations arising.

160. On the other hand, the Court reiterates that some participating States in the framework of this procedure expressly stated their approach that there is no uniform position in the Latin American sub-region to conclude that diplomatic asylum is part of regional custom, and that it is only a treaty-based system. Furthermore, most participating States argued that there is no legal obligation to grant diplomatic asylum, as it constitutes an act of foreign policy.

161. In addition, despite the fact that the United States of America has in practice granted protection in its embassies in specific cases, it has persistently opposed it since 1933 when, at the Seventh International American Conference in Montevideo, it stated that, "by virtue of the fact that the United States of America does not recognize or subscribe to the doctrine of political asylum as part of international law, the Delegation of the United States of America abstains from signing this Convention".

162. Thus, the Court finds that the element of *opinio juris* necessary for the determination of a customary rule is not present, notwithstanding the State practice of granting diplomatic asylum in certain situations or granting some form of protection in their legations.

163. The granting of diplomatic asylum and its scope must therefore be governed by the inter- State conventions governing it and by domestic legislation. That is, those States that have signed multilateral or bilateral agreements on diplomatic asylum, or that have it recognized as a fundamental right in their domestic legislation, are bound by the terms established in those regulations. In this regard, the Court considers it appropriate to stress that States have the power to grant diplomatic asylum as an expression of their sovereignty, which is in line with the logic of the so-called "Latin American tradition of asylum". . . .

[In response to Question B] 172. Thus, the Court has affirmed that, in accordance with the rules of treaty interpretation, as well as those specific to the American Convention, the ordinary meaning of the term jurisdiction, interpreted in good faith and taking into account the context, purpose and intent of the American Convention, indicates that the scope of the general obligations is not limited to the concept of national territory, but has effect with respect to certain forms of exercise of jurisdiction outside the territory of the State in question.

173. Therefore, the margin of protection for the rights recognized in the American Convention is wide, in that the obligations of the State Parties are not restricted to the geographic space corresponding to their territory, but

rather includes those situations where, even outside the territory of a State, a person is under its jurisdiction. Therefore, for the Court, the "jurisdiction" referred to in Article 1(1) of the American Convention provides for circumstances in which extraterritorial conduct by States constitutes an exercise of jurisdiction by that State.

177. In view of the foregoing, the Court concludes that host States are bound by the provisions of Article 1(1) of the Convention, insofar as they are exercising control, authority or responsibility over any person, whether that person is on the land, water, sea or air territory of that State. Therefore, the Court considers that the general obligations established by the American Convention are applicable to the actions of diplomatic agents deployed in the territory of third States, provided that the personal link of jurisdiction with the person concerned can be established. . . .

[In response to Question C] 192. [T]he principle of *non-refoulement* is enforceable by any foreign person, including those seeking international protection, over whom the State in question is exercising authority or who is under its effective control, whether on the State's land, river, sea or air.

194. It follows from the foregoing that, within the framework of the principle of *non-refoulement*, certain specific obligations, in terms of individualized risk assessment and appropriate protective measures, including measures against arbitrary detention, are required of the host State, under whose jurisdiction the person who has applied for protection in a diplomatic mission is situated. In this regard, the Court recalls that "it is not enough for States to refrain from violating this principle, it is imperative that positive measures be taken." . . .

[The Court decides] . . .

2. Within the framework of the inter-American system the right to seek and receive asylum is configured as a human right to seek and receive international protection in a foreign territory, including refugee status according to the relevant United Nations instruments or the corresponding national laws, and territorial asylum according to the various inter-American conventions on the subject. . . .

3. Diplomatic asylum is not protected under Article 22.7 of the American Convention on Human Rights or Article XXVII of the American Declaration of the Rights and Duties of Man, and must therefore be governed by the inter-State conventions that regulate it and domestic legislation provisions. . . .

4. The principle of *non-refoulement* is enforceable for any foreign person, including those seeking international protection, over whom the State concerned is exercising authority or which is under its effective control, regardless of whether he or she is on the State's land, river, sea or air territory. . . .

5. The principle of *non-refoulement* not only requires that the person not be returned, but also imposes positive obligations on States. . . .

A couple months after the advisory opinion was issued, Assange, the founder of Wikileaks, sued the Government of Ecuador indicating that his rights as an Ecuadorian citizen would be violated if internal rules are imposed on him including eliminating his internet connection and forcing him to leave the embassy. The Ecuadorian court dismissed the case.

d.   Other Courts

1.   *World Trade Organization Dispute Body*

In light of the tariffs announced by the U.S. government, the World Trade Organization Dispute Body faces an unprecedented number of cases. A list of the cases that have yet to be decided as of 2019 include:

(1) DS544 China v. United States—Certain Measures on Steel and Aluminum Products
(2) DS547 India v. United States—Certain Measures on Steel and Aluminum Products
(3) DS548 European Union v. United States—Certain Measures on Steel and Aluminum Products
(4) DS550 Canada v. United States—Certain Measures on Steel and Aluminum Products
(5) DS551 Mexico v. United States—Certain Measures on Steel and Aluminum Products
(6) DS552 Norway v. United States—Certain Measures on Steel and Aluminum Products
(7) DS554 Russian Federation v. United States—Certain Measures on Steel and Aluminum Products
(8) DS556 Switzerland v. United States—Certain Measures on Steel and Aluminum Products
(9) DS564 Turkey v. United States—Certain Measures on Steel and Aluminum Products

In most of these cases, the United States has brought counterclaims on the additional duties that have been levied on U.S. goods. The Appellate Body of the World Trade Organization has nearly become defunct with a deadlock in appointing new members leading to only 3 members sitting out of a panel of 7. An informal process was launched in December 2018 to address the impasse.

2.   *United Nations Human Rights Committee*

In October 2018, the Human Rights Committee decided that France had violated the human rights of two women who had been criminally banned in France from wearing an Islamic veil that covers all of the face except the eyes.[29] The decision that the law violated freedom of religion was made after two complaints were filed in 2016 on the basis of prosecutions in 2012. The Committee concluded that while the State could require that individual show their faces for identification purposes for security reasons, a general ban was not necessary to achieve this outcome. France was directed to compensate the women and review its legislation.

3. Extraordinary Chambers in the Court of Cambodia

The Khmer Rouge took power in 1975 in Cambodia and were ousted in 1979 after approximately 1.7 million people died of starvation, torture, execution, and forced labor. In 2001, the government of Cambodia created a court to try perpetrators of crimes against humanity called the Extraordinary Chambers in the Court of Cambodia (ECCC). The court is a Cambodian court with international participation that applies international standards to charge senior leaders of Democratic Kampuchea or those believed to be responsible for grave violations of national and international law. The Court has had four matters before it—only one of which has been fully decided to date. On November 16, 2018, the ECCC delivered its judgment in Case 002/02, convicting former senior Khmer Rouge leaders Nuon Chea and Khieu Samphan of genocide, additional crimes against humanity, and grave breaches of the Geneva Conventions and sentencing them to life in prison.[30] Case 002/01 had already found Nuon Chea and Khieu Samphan guilty of crimes against humanity resulting in life imprisonment.

4. The International Residual Mechanism for Criminal Tribunal

Established by Security Council Resolution in 1966 (2010) to complete the work of the International Criminal Tribunal for Rwanda and the International Criminal Tribunal for the Former Yugoslavia, the Appeals Chamber issued its second judgment on April 11, 2018.[31] In this judgment, the court reversed the acquittal of Vojislav Seselj for crimes against humanity. Sentencing Mr. Seselj to ten years imprisonment, the Chamber found that there was ample evidence to support a finding that there were

29. Human Rights Committee, CCPR/C/123/D/2747/2016 https://tbinternet.ohchr.org/_layouts/treatybodyexternal/Download.aspx?symbolno=CCPR/C/123/D/2747/2016&Lang=en and Human Rights Committee, CCPR/C/123/D/2807/2016 https://tbinternet.ohchr.org/_layouts/treatybodyexternal/Download.aspx?symbolno=CCPR/C/123/D/2807/2016&Lang=en.

30. Trial Chamber Summary of Judgment in Case O02/02 https://www.eccc.gov.kh/sites/default/files/documents/courtdoc/%5Bdate-in-tz%5D/20181119%20Summary%20of%20Judgement%20Case%20002-02%20ENG_checked%20against%20delivery_amended%20a.pdf.

31. IRMCT, ŠEŠELJ, VOJISLAV (MICT-16-99), http://www.irmct.org/en/cases/mict-16-99.

systematic attacks against non-Serbian civilian populations in Croatia, Bosnia, and Herzegovina.

5. Investor State Arbitration

The International Center for the Settlement of Investment Disputes (ICSID) facilitated numerous investor-state arbitrations in 2018. One case worth mentioning is Vattenfall v. Germany involving a Swedish investor whose nuclear investments in Germany were shuttered when the government decided to phase out nuclear power shortly after the nuclear disaster at Japan's Fukushima plant in March 2011.[32] The Swedish company claimed expropriation, and the German government claimed that the ICSID tribunal did not have jurisdiction. Germany's argument was based on a European Court of Justice decision finding that arbitration proceedings were invalid if it involved an EU member state and a company based in an EU state. The ICSID tribunal rejected Germany's argument and found that it could proceed to hear the case.

Another case worth mentioning is a case involving the government of Serbia. The tribunal held that Serbia had denied fair and equitable treatment to a Belgian waste management company and its Serbian subsidiary because the Serbian government had failed to equally enforce its environmental laws against wholly owned Serbian companies competing in the market.[33]

VI. Violations of Humanitarian Law

In 2018, the international community focused political attention on a number of areas involving ongoing armed conflicts. In some of these areas, the situation for civilians has become increasingly perilous. This section will highlight international legal responses in Yemen that have been characterized as the worst humanitarian crisis that the world has seen in terms of numbers of displaced civilians.

In 2018, the humanitarian situation in Yemen declined precipitously. Yemen continued to serve as the proxy war between Saudi Arabia and Iran. Yemen is considered to be engaged in non-international armed conflict. By some accounts, because of the ongoing fighting, Yemen is on the verge of imminent collapse given that out of a population of 28 million, 22.2 million

---

32. Vattenfall v. Germany, ICSID Case No. ARB/12/12, Decision on the Achmea Issue, (August 31, 2018) https://www.italaw.com/sites/default/files/case-documents/italaw9916.pdf.

33. Serbia Held Liable at ICSID in Case Alleging Failure to Enforce Environmental Regulations   https://www.iareporter.com/articles/serbia-held-liable-at-icsid-in-case-alleging-failure-to-enforce-environmental-regulations/.

are in need of humanitarian aid, 19 million lack clean water, 16.4 million lack access to healthcare, and 14 million are at risk of famine. In April 2018, the United Nations issued a report detailing the possibility of violations of international humanitarian law. The Government of Yemen and its coalition, including Saudi Arabia and the United Arab Emirates, may have violated international humanitarian law for the sick and wounded by closing down the Sana'a Airport, and Yemeni civilians by targeting civilian events including funerals and weddings.[34] Findings from the report are excerpted here:

[Findings on civilian targeting]

Based on the incidents examined, and information received in relation to the targeting process, the Group of Experts have reasonable grounds to believe the following

(a) In the absence of any apparent military objective in the vicinity, the objects struck raise serious concerns about the respect of the principle of distinction and how military targets were defined and selected. The use of precision-guided munitions would normally indicate that the object struck was the target;

(b) The number of civilian casualties raises serious concerns as to the nature and effectiveness of any proportionality assessments conducted;

(c) The timing of some attacks and the choice of weapons raise serious concerns as to the nature and effectiveness of any precautionary measures adopted;

(d) The failure to ensure that all relevant commanders have access to the no-strike list raises serious concerns about the ability of the coalition to comply with the special protections accorded to such objects;

(e) The use in some cases of "double strikes" close in time, which affect first responders, raises serious concerns as to whether updated proportionality assessments and precautionary measures were carried out for the second strikes.[35]

The report concluded that the experts had "reasonable grounds to believe that the parties to the armed conflict in Yemen have committed a substantial number of violations of international humanitarian law." The experts offered the following specific recommendations for parties to conflict:[36]

(a) Immediately cease acts of violence committed against civilians in violation of applicable international human rights and international humanitarian

34. Situation of human rights in Yemen, including violations and abuses since 2014. Report of the United Nations High Commissioner for Human Rights containing the findings of the Group of Independent Eminent International and Regional Experts and a summary of technical assistance provided by the Office of the High Commissioner to the National Commission of InquiryA/HRC/39/43 (August 7, 2018) https://www.ohchr.org/Documents/Countries/YE/A_HRC_39_43_EN.docx.

35. Id. at para. 38.

36. Id. at para. 111.

law, take all feasible precautions to protect civilians from the effects of hostilities and meet the basic needs of the civilian population, in particular women and children;

(b) Respect international humanitarian law, including in relation to the prohibition on attacks against civilians and civilian objects, and the core principles of distinction, proportionality and precaution;

(c) Take the necessary measures to remove disproportionate restrictions on the safe and expeditious entry into Yemen of humanitarian supplies and other goods indispensable to the civilian population, and the movement of persons including through Sana'a International Airport;

(d) Fulfil obligations to facilitate the rapid and unimpeded passage of humanitarian relief and unhindered access to medical facilities both in Yemen and abroad;

(e) Ensure that all persons deprived of their liberty have their detention reviewed by a judge in compliance with national and international law;

(f) Ensure that arrests of individuals in connection with the ongoing conflict are carried out on legal grounds only and supported by credible and sufficient evidence;

(g) Document all unofficial detention centres and transfer detainees to official detention facilities in line with national and international law;

(h) Create a national register for missing persons and inform families of the whereabouts of all detainees;

(i) Immediately cease all attacks against freedoms of expression and of belief, including detention, enforced disappearance and intimidation, and release all journalists and others detained for exercising their freedom of expression or belief;

(j) Cease acts of sexual and gender-based violence in all forms, including sexual violence against women and children, sexual violence in detention and the persecution of women activists;

(k) Conduct transparent, independent, impartial and effective gender-sensitive investigations of all violations and crimes in accordance with international standards, to ensure accountability for the perpetrators and justice for the victims;

(l) Cease and prevent the recruitment and use of children in the armed conflict;

(m) Establish an independent and competent mechanism to ensure the identification, release, recovery and reintegration of all children, including girls, who have been recruited or used in hostilities by all parties to the conflict.

In December 2018, the UN Secretary General issued a statement that "reminds the parties that a negotiated political settlement through inclusive intra-Yemeni dialogue is the only way to end the conflict and address the ongoing humanitarian crisis."[37] An agreement was signed in Sweden on December 13, 2018, committing the Houthi rebels to withdraw their forces from Hudaydah, the main conduit for humanitarian aid entering Yemen, and to implement a cease-fire in the surrounding province. [38]

VII. Human Rights

On December 10, 2018, the international community celebrated the 70th anniversary of the adoption of the 30 articles of the Universal Declaration of Human Rights. Even as the Preamble to the declaration acknowledges that the "[r]ecognition of the inherent dignity and of the equal and inalienable rights of all members of the human family is the foundation of freedom, justice and peace in the world", communities face an increasingly varied set of human rights challenges. This section highlights 2018 developments in a few prominent human rights areas.

a. General Comment No 36 (2018) on Article 6 of the International Covenant on Civil and Political Rights, on the Right to Life

The UN Human Rights Committee publishes its interpretation of the provisions of the ICCPR in the form of "general comments." The last general comments on Article 6, which recognizes and protects the right to life all human beings, were published in 1982 and 1984. Comment No. 36 replaces those comments.[39] Excerpts are provided below:

> 3. The right to life is a right which should not be interpreted narrowly. It concerns the entitlement of individuals to be free from acts and omissions that are intended or may be expected to cause their unnatural or premature death, as well as to enjoy a life with dignity. Article 6 guarantees this right for all human beings, without distinction of any kind, including for persons suspected or convicted of even the most serious crimes. . . .

37. Statement attributable to the Spokesman for the Secretary-General on Yemen, Stéphane Dujarric, Spokesman for the Secretary-General (December 6, 2018) https://www.un.org/sg/en/content/sg/statement/2018-12-06/statement-attributable-spokesman-secretary-general-yemen.

38. UN Office of the Special Envoy of the Secretary-General to Yemen, Stockholm Agreement, December 13, 2018 https://osesgy.unmissions.org/full-text-stockholm-agreement.

39. Human Rights Committee, General Comment No 36 (2018) on Article 6 of the International Covenant on Civil and Political Rights, on the Right to Life CCPR/C/GC/36 (October 30, 2018), https://tbinternet.ohchr.org/Treaties/CCPR/Shared%20Documents/1_Global/CCPR_C_GC_36_8785_E.pdf.

5. Paragraphs 2, 4, 5, and 6 of Article 6 of the Covenant set out specific safeguards for ensuring that in States parties which have not yet abolished the death penalty, it must not be applied except for the most serious crimes, and then only in the most exceptional cases and under the strictest limits. The prohibition on arbitrary deprivation of life contained in article 6, paragraph 1 further limits the ability of States parties to apply the death penalty. . . .

8. Although States parties may adopt measures designed to regulate voluntary terminations of pregnancy, such measures must not result in violation of the right to life of a pregnant woman or girl, or her other rights under the Covenant. Thus, restrictions on the ability of women or girls to seek abortion must not, inter alia, jeopardize their lives, subject them to physical or mental pain or suffering which violates article 7, discriminate against them or arbitrarily interfere with their privacy. States parties must provide safe, legal, and effective access to abortion where the life and health of the pregnant woman or girl is at risk, or where carrying a pregnancy to term would cause the pregnant woman or girl substantial pain or suffering, most notably where the pregnancy is the result of rape or incest or is not viable. In addition, States parties may not regulate pregnancy or abortion in all other cases in a manner than runs contrary to their duty to ensure that women and girls do not have to undertake unsafe abortions, and they should revise their abortion laws accordingly. . . .

9. While acknowledging the central importance to human dignity of personal autonomy, States should take adequate measures, without violating their other Covenant obligations, to prevent suicides, especially among individuals in particularly vulnerable situations, including individuals deprived of their liberty. States parties that allow medical professionals to provide medical treatment or the medical means in order to facilitate the termination of life of afflicted adults, such as the terminally ill, who experience severe physical or mental pain and suffering and wish to die with dignity, must ensure the existence of robust legal and institutional safeguards to verify that medical professionals are complying with the free, informed, explicit and, unambiguous decision of their patients, with a view to protecting patients from pressure and abuse. . . .

The Prohibition against Arbitrary Deprivation of Life . . .

12. . . . In order not to be qualified as arbitrary under article 6, the application of potentially lethal force by a private person acting in self-defense, or by another person coming to his or her defence, must be strictly necessary in view of the threat posed by the attacker; it must represent a method of last resort after other alternatives have been exhausted or deemed inadequate; the amount of force applied cannot exceed the amount strictly needed for responding to the threat; the force applied must be carefully directed-only against the attacker and the threat responded to must involve imminent death or serious injury. The use of potentially lethal force for law enforcement purposes is an extreme measure, which should be resorted to only when strictly necessary in order to protect life or prevent serious injury from an imminent threat. . . .

20. State parties must enact a protective legal framework, which includes effective criminal prohibitions on all manifestations of violence or incitement

to violence that are likely to result in a deprivation of life, such as intentional and negligent homicide, unnecessary or disproportionate use of firearms, infanticide, 'honour' killings, lynchings, violent hate crimes, blood feuds, ritual kills, death threats, and terrorist attacks. . . .

21. . . . States parties are thus under a due diligence obligation to undertake reasonable positive measures, which do not impose on them disproportionate burdens, in response to reasonably foreseeable threats to life originating from private persons and entities, whose conduct is not attributable to the State. Hence, States parties are obliged to take adequate preventive measures in order to protect individuals against reasonably foreseen threats of being murdered or killed by criminals and organized crime or militia groups, including armed or terrorist groups. States parties should also disband irregular armed groups such as private armies and vigilante groups, that are responsible for deprivations of life and reduce the proliferation of potentially lethal weapons to unauthorized individuals. States parties must further take adequate measures of protection, including continuous supervision, in order to prevent, investigate, punish and remedy arbitrary deprivation of life by private entities, such as private transportation companies, private hospitals and private security firms.

22. States parties must take appropriate measures to protect individuals against deprivation of life by other States, international organizations and foreign corporations operating within their territory or in other areas subject to their jurisdiction. They must also take appropriate legislative and other measures to ensure that all activities taking place in whole or in part within their territory and in other places subject to their jurisdiction, but having a direct and reasonably foreseeable impact on the right to life of individuals outside their territory, including activities taken by corporate entities based in their territory or subject to their jurisdiction, are consistent with article 6, taking national standards of corporate responsibility, and of the right of victims to obtain an effective remedy. . . .

23. The duty to protect the right to life requires States parties to take special measures of protection towards persons in situation of vulnerability whose lives have been placed at particular risk because of specific threats or pre-existing patterns of violence. These include human rights defenders, officials fighting corruption and organized crime, humanitarian workers, journalists, prominent public figures, witnesses to crime, and victims of domestic and gender-based violence and human trafficking. They may also include children, especially children in street situations, unaccompanied migrant children and children in situations of armed conflict, members of ethnic and religious minorities and indigenous peoples, lesbian, gay, bisexual, transgender and intersex (LGBTI) persons, persons with albinism, alleged witches, displaced persons, asylum seekers, refugees and stateless persons. . . .

26. The duty to protect life also implies that States parties should take appropriate measures to address the general conditions in society that may give rise to direct threats to life or prevent individuals from enjoying their right to life with dignity. These general conditions may include high levels of criminal

and gun violence, pervasive traffic and industrial accidents, degradation of the environment, deprivation of land, territories and resources of indigenous peoples, the prevalence of life threatening diseases, such as AIDS, tuberculosis or malaria, extensive substance abuse, widespread hunger and malnutrition and extreme poverty and homelessness. The measures called for addressing adequate conditions for protecting the right to life include, where necessary, measures designed to ensure access without delay by individuals to essential goods and services such as food, water, shelter, health-care, electricity and sanitation, and other measures designed to promote and facilitate adequate general conditions such as the bolstering of effective emergency health services, emergency response operations (including fire-fighters, ambulances and police forces) and social housing programs. . . . Furthermore, States parties should also develop, when necessary, contingency plans and disaster management plans designed to increase preparedness and address natural and man-made disasters, which may adversely affect enjoyment of the right to life, such as hurricanes, tsunamis, earthquakes, radioactive accidents and massive cyberattacks resulting in disruption of essential services. . . .

62. Environmental degradation, climate change and unsustainable development constitute some of the most pressing and serious threats to the ability of present and future generations to enjoy the right to life. Obligations of States parties under international environmental law should thus inform the contents of article 6 of the Covenant, and the obligation of States parties to respect and ensure the right to life should also inform their relevant obligations under international environmental law. Implementation of the obligation to respect and ensure the right to life, and in particular life with dignity, depends, inter alia, on measures taken by States parties to preserve the environment and protect it against harm, pollution and climate change caused by public and private actors. States parties should therefore ensure sustainable use of natural resources, develop and implement substantive environmental standards, conduct environmental impact assessments and consult with relevant States about activities likely to have a significant impact on the environment, provide notification to other States concerned about natural disasters and emergencies and cooperate with them, provide appropriate access to information on environmental hazards and pay due regard to the precautionary approach.

b. Discrimination Against Women and Protection of Women Human Rights Defenders

In May 2018, the United Nations made public a report "on the issue of discrimination against women in law and in practice".[40] This report was based

40. Human Rights Council, Report of the Working Group on the issue of discrimination against women in law and in practice, A/HRC/38/46 (May 14, 2018) https://reliefweb.int/sites/reliefweb.int/files/resources/G1813285.pdf.

on evaluating the work of the United Nations toward achieving civil political, economic, social, and cultural rights for all to ensure inclusion of half
of the world population. Among the observations in the report, the group
observed that certain concepts such as "complementarity", "equity", and
"protection of the family" have been "employed to justify State and non-
State violations" of rights to equality and nondiscrimination by women.[41]
The Working Group observes that "40 years after the adoption by the
General Assembly of the Convention on the Elimination of All Forms of
Discrimination against Women no country in the world has successfully
eliminated discrimination against women or achieved full equality."[42]

The report offers some successes for reducing gender-based discrimination, identifies number of areas where legal challenges remain, and
proposes a new work plan on emerging issues related to protection of fundamental human rights for women:

1. ACKNOWLEDGING PROGRESS MADE IN ADVANCING GENDER EQUALITY

18. International commitment to fulfilling women's right to political participation has grown substantially. Over the course of the twentieth century, wom-
en's right to vote has been almost universally implemented. In fewer than two
decades after the Fourth World Conference on Women: Action for Equality,
Development and Peace, held in Beijing, the global average for women's political representation has doubled. The introduction of quotas in some countries
that were undergoing political transition resulted in significant increases in
women's parliamentary representation. Positive trends have also been seen in
terms of extending special measures and affirmative action to other areas of
public life beyond parliamentary representation (see A/HRC/23/50).

19. In recent years, women demanding dignity and rights have marched
worldwide and have increasingly used social media to take action. Technology
has enabled new forms of women's political expression and engagement.
Movements denouncing gender-based violence against women, such as
#NiUnaMenos and #MeToo, have swept much of the globe, following
decades of advocacy from women's rights movements demanding an end
to violence against women in environments that normalize discrimination
against women. Gender-based violence is one of the worst manifestations of
such discrimination.

20. Significant progress has been made in closing the gender gap in education, and women have increasingly participated in the cultural and scientific
lives of their communities and nations. Women's labor force participation
has increased significantly and women entrepreneurs in small and medium-
sized enterprises have made considerable contributions as crucial economic

41. Id. at para. 13.
42. Id. at para. 16

actors. Initial efforts have been made by some countries to increase women's participation in economic and financial leadership by imposing gender quota requirements for corporate boards. Moreover, in times of crisis, some countries have chosen alternatives to austerity measures to ensure women's continued economic inclusion (see A/HRC/26/39).

21. The right of women and girls to equality in the family has been recognized in international human rights law and guaranteed in most modern legal regimes, which have reformed family law systems to enshrine gender equality. In some countries, progress has been made in challenging gender stereotypes and the unequal roles and responsibilities attributed to women and men in the family. A considerable number of countries have developed laws criminalizing domestic violence and providing protection for victims (see A/HRC/29/40). . . .

23. An impressive body of regional and international human rights standards has been developed over the past few decades, in which recognition and protection of women's right to equality has been central and prioritized. Considerable progress has been made in the number of national constitutions guaranteeing gender equality and laws enacted to prohibit sex discrimination and gender-based violence. . . .

24. Despite these achievements made over long years of struggle, discrimination against women and impunity for the violation of women's rights persist in both the private and public spheres, in times of conflict as in times of peace, and in all regions of the world. Not only is the advancement of women's rights and full equality too slow, uneven and far from a global reality (see E/CN.6/2015/3), but women's hard-fought achievements now risk being reversed. An unprecedented pushback has been progressing across regions by an alliance of conservative political ideologies and religious fundamentalisms. Retrogressions have been occurring, often in the name of culture, religion and traditions, and threaten the hard-fought progress in achieving women's equality.

2. DEADLOCKS, RETROGRESSIONS AND BACKLASHES

FAMILY AND CULTURE

25. In its reports, the Working Group has demonstrated the persistence of a global discriminatory cultural construction of gender, often tied to religion, and the continued reliance of States on cultural justifications for adopting discriminatory laws or for failing to respect international human rights law and standards. It has particularly emphasized that failure to ensure the equality of women and girls within the family undermines any attempt to ensure their equality in all areas of society (see A/HRC/29/40).

26. Throughout its work, the Working Group has shown that discrimination against women and girls and the backlash against their rights all too often start in the family where, for example, women and girls are undervalued,

may be limited to certain roles, experience harmful practices and patriarchal oppression, and suffer other human rights abuses, including domestic violence and sexual abuse. As indicated by the Working Group, although discriminatory laws governing family life have been repealed in most countries, such laws are still in force in a few others (ibid.). In some countries, women are deprived of their fundamental rights due to, inter alia, a lower minimum age of marriage for girls, guardianship systems, forced marriage, polygamous marriage, discrimination in nationality rights, divorce rights and unequal rights to custody, inheritance and access to property and land. In the name of perceived honour, purity and tradition, girls and women are subject to "honour" killing, child marriage, widowhood rites and female genital mutilation, among other violations of their rights. In some regions, there has been no progress at all towards eliminating child marriage.

27. . . . One extremely revealing fact is the high number of reservations to the Convention on the Elimination of All Forms of Discrimination against Women, particularly to article 16 on equality in the family,11 in which States deny women's and girls' right to equality in deference to religious norms, and refute their accountability for the universal applicability of human rights (see A/HRC/29/40). This also shows that equality in the private domain—the family—remains one of the biggest hurdles to achieving gender equality.

28. Under the guise of protecting the family, some States are taking initiatives aimed at further diluting human rights. While recognizing that the family is the fundamental group unit of society and is entitled to protection, the Working Group insists on the need to reassert women's right to equality in all aspects of family life and to recognize that diverse forms of family exist. Protection of the family cannot be used as a justification for laws, policies or practices that would deny women and girls their full and equal human rights (ibid.). The advancement of women and girls depends on the recognition in law and in practice of their right to equality as members of communities and families. . . .

30. While the Working Group is committed to the principle of upholding freedom of religion or belief as human rights to be protected, it regrets the increasing challenges to gender equality in the name of religion. It joins other international human rights expert mechanisms in reiterating that freedom of religion or belief should never be used to justify discrimination against women (see A/HRC/29/40). . . .

ECONOMIC AND SOCIAL PARTICIPATION

38. In its reports, the Working Group has demonstrated how women still face structural disadvantages and discrimination in the economic and social spheres throughout their life cycle. Social and cultural barriers still prevent many girls from completing their education, and legal discrimination, entrenched inequalities in wages and labor force participation and caring responsibilities prevent women from participating equally in economic and social life. . . .

39. Indeed, women continue to be paid less than men for work of equal value and are severely underrepresented in top leadership in decision-making

bodies in business, finance and trade, including in international institutions such as the International Monetary Fund and the World Trade Organization, and in cooperatives and trade unions. Furthermore, women have been grossly underrepresented in the formulation of the macroeconomic policies that have led to rocketing inequality, austerity measures and the undermining of care services on which women are more dependent than men. Today, there are more girls in schools than ever before, but one out of five adolescent girls is still out of school. Moreover, women's higher educational achievements worldwide have not always translated into corresponding leadership positions or even equality in the economic field. While more women have entered the workforce, they still represent only 49 per cent of working age women, against 75 per cent of working age men. Globally, the gender pay gap still stands at 23 per cent. Women often have access only to vulnerable forms of employment; the majority of women in developing countries are employed in the informal sector or in family businesses, and do not always receive wages directly. In countries where women's income mainly comes from agricultural activities, they generally have very limited ownership of land. . . .

90. The Working Group recommends that States:

(a) Give the issue of women's right to equality high visibility and top political priority;

(b) Systematically integrate into legislation and policy the recommendations contained in the Working Group's thematic and country reports and its communications in order to ensure that obligations to eliminate discrimination against women are met;

(c) Repeal all discriminatory laws and practices, including those that discriminate against women on traditional, cultural or religious grounds and laws that exclusively or disproportionately criminalize action or behavior by women and girls, taking into account the multiple and intersecting forms of discrimination faced by many women and girls;

(d) Give priority to establishing, strengthening and investing in institutions devoted to the advancement of women's rights and gender equality;

(e) Create an enabling, supportive environment for civil society and other stakeholders to combat the backlash against women's human rights and to resist all anti-rights trends and movements with a definitive response grounded in binding human rights obligations, with women's and girls' rights at the center;

(f) Counter the narratives around gender ideology used by conservative lobbies to misinform societies and undermine the advancement of women's rights and gender equality;

(g) Promote recognition of the fact that cultural, religious and family values are not incompatible with women's and girls' human rights, and recognize the equality of women and girls as a fundamental tenet of international human rights law that must be protected, respected and fulfilled in all States and at all levels of society, including within the family;

(h) Continue promoting and protecting the fundamental principle that all rights are universal, indivisible, interdependent and interrelated;

(i) Ensure respect for women's rights to make decisions about their own bodies and to receive comprehensive sexuality education so they can enjoy their right to sexual and reproductive health, including safe, legal and affordable access to contraception and termination of pregnancy;

(j) Establish parity, including through temporary special measures, to ensure equal representation of women in public, political and economic decision-making and leadership;

(k) Develop strategies to increase women's access to decent work and achieve equal pay;

(l) Ensure social protection floors for care work, which would facilitate the participation of women equally with men in economic and social activities;

(m) Institute measures to combat discriminatory social norms and harmful stereotypes about women's and girls' bodies, roles and capabilities.

In a number of conflict zones, women human rights defenders have been subject to prejudice and violence. In promoting human rights law, these women are often excluded from peace processes, may be subject to criminal law for their protests, and have become victims of gender-based violence when they speak out. For example, counterterrorism laws in some regions such as the Middle East and North Africa have been used to silence women. In some places, particularly where there are lucrative extractive industries, both State actors and non-State actors threaten women human rights defenders with impunity. On November 29, International Women Human Rights Defenders Day, the United Nations called for:[43]

1. Public recognition by the highest State authorities of the importance and legitimacy of their work, and a commitment to protect them against violence or threats;
2. Repeal of any State legislation or elimination of any measures to penalize or obstruct their work;
3. State institutions safeguarding their work to be strengthened;
4. Investigating and punishing any form of violence or threat against them; and
5. Due diligence of States to protect women human rights defenders that are threatened by non-State actors.

43. United Nations Office of the High Commissioner, Women human rights defenders must be protected, say UN experts (November 29, 2018), https://www.ohchr.org/EN/NewsEvents/Pages/DisplayNews.aspx?NewsID=23943&LangID=E.

c. Environmental Defenders

Environmental defenders include individuals and groups who defend environmental rights such as the right to a clean and healthy enforcement. Because of rampant corruption, weak government enforcement, and impunity for the actors, individuals and groups—particularly in the Global South—are at risk of being killed or being the victims of violence because of their efforts to uphold their rights. In March 2018, the UN Environment drafted a UN Policy "Promoting Greater Protection for Environmental Defenders" including denouncing attacks, advocating for protection of environmental rights and protection of environmental rights defenders, supporting the "environmental rule of law", and requesting government accountability. The following is a public statement from the Head of UN Environment regarding the death of a land rights activist and two indigenous leaders.

> UN Environment notes with deep concern the escalation of violence against land rights activists in Brazil. The recent murder of Nazildo dos Santos and two other environmental activists in the state of Pará is indicative of a worrying pattern of retaliation against those protecting their environmental and human rights.
>
> Land rights which are guaranteed under the Brazilian constitution must be fulfilled by government and respected by business. The murder of indigenous people living on the frontlines of environmental protection is unacceptable. UN Environment calls for a full, impartial and transparent investigation into the murder of Nazildo dos Santos Brito and of the two leaders of the Association of Caboclos Indígenas e Quilombolas da Amazônia killed since December.
>
> This violence in the heart of one of the most ecologically important places on earth mars the many advances Brazil has made in recent years to safeguard its natural resources from unsustainable use. Solutions to land rights challenges are available and have been implemented in many parts of the world, but space must be made available to indigenous and local communities to speak on issues intrinsic to their environmental and human rights. UN Environment has been successfully engaging with the Roundtable on Sustainable Palmoil to promote the sustainable production of palm oil. We are available to engage with relevant authorities from the state of Para, as well as palm oil producers from the region, on the issue of palm oil and land rights.
>
> UN Environment promotes greater protection for defenders and recognizes and relies on the critical work of the UN Special Procedures and civil society actors. This policy is grounded in international environmental law, including in relevant UN instruments and resolutions. It is on this basis that UN Environment is calling for the violence against land rights activists to cease

with immediate effect and the safety of the leaders of land rights groups be assured.

Erik Solheim
Head, UN Environment[44]

On March 4, 2018, 24 countries adopted the Regional Agreement on Access to Information, Public Participation and Access to Justice in Environmental Matters in Latin America and the Caribbean (the Escazu Agreement).[45] The Agreement included the follow text to enhance protection of human rights defenders working to protect the environment.

ARTICLE 9

Human Rights Defenders in Environmental Matters

1. Each Party shall guarantee a safe and enabling environment for persons, groups and organizations that promote and defend human rights in environmental matters, so that they are able to act free from threat, restriction and insecurity.

2. Each Party shall take adequate and effective measures to recognize, protect and promote all the rights of human rights defenders in environmental matters, including their right to life, personal integrity, freedom of opinion and expression, peaceful assembly and association, and free movement, as well as their ability to exercise their access rights, taking into account its international obligations in the field of human rights, its constitutional principles and the basic concepts of its legal system.

3. Each Party shall also take appropriate, effective and timely measures to prevent, investigate and punish attacks, threats or intimidations that human rights defenders in environmental matters may suffer while exercising the rights set out in the present Agreement.

Some States have prosecuted perpetrators of crimes against environmental defenders. In November 2018, the Sentencing Tribunal of the Honduran Judiciary in Tegucigalpa convicted seven men in the murder of indigenous rights activist Berta Caceres, who had been protesting a joint development hydroelectric dam that would deprive the indigenous

44. Statement in Response to the Murder of Environmental Campaigner Nazildo dos Santos Brito (April 24, 2018) https://www.unenvironment.org/news-and-stories/statement/statement-response-murder-environmental-campaigner-nazildo-dos-santos.
45. Escazu Agreement http://repositorio.cepal.org/bitstream/handle/11362/43583/1/S1800428_en.pdf.

community of food sources. Two UN Special Rapporteurs continued to express their concern that the masterminds of Ms. Caceres's murder had not yet been brought to justice.[46] In October 2018, Peru arrested 12 individuals who are alleged to have killed four environmental defenders protecting Peru's first private nature reserve, the Chaparri Ecological Reserve, from development of a water reservoir. The community's ecotourism efforts to protect dry tropical forest have been threatened by land squatters lured by the possibility of local government built agricultural water reservoirs.

d.   Right to Adequate Housing

Approximately one quarter of the world's urban population lives in informal settlements that often lack sanitation and clean water. States have committed to upgrading these settlements by 2030 in the Sustainable Development Goals (Goal 11). The Special Rapporteur on Adequate Housing proposed that States do not simply remove these informal settlements but work closely with the capacities of residents in these areas to ensure protection of not just the right to housing but also the right to participation in and access to justice. In the report, the Rapporteur offers the following observations and recommendations including acknowledging residents of informal settlements who oppose removal by the government as human rights defenders:[47]

> 4. While Agenda 2030 refers to "slums", the Special Rapporteur prefers the term "informal settlements" as one that is more in keeping with a human rights-based approach to housing. The term "slum" is often considered pejorative and stigmatizing and has generally led to bad policy: "slums" are often viewed as a problem requiring "clearance", rather than as communities to be supported. Households reported by governments as having been "upgraded" have often been warehoused in housing blocks devoid of dignity, culture or community, or displaced to outlying urban wastelands with no access to work, social ties, transportation or services.

> 5. The present report proposes a radically different approach centered on the right to housing. It understands that informality is created and exacerbated by the imposition of a particular system of laws, private markets, planning and resource allocation that neglects and violates the fundamental rights of those who have no choice but to rely on informal settlements. . . .

46. United Nations Human Rights Office of the High Commissioner, Honduras: Masterminds of Berta Cáceres killing still at large, say UN experts (December 7, 2018) https://www.ohchr.org/EN/NewsEvents/Pages/DisplayNews.aspx?NewsID=23994&LangID=E.

47. UN General Assembly, Report of the Special Rapporteur on Adequate Housing as a Component of the Right to an Adequate Standard of Living, and on the Right of Non-Discrimination in this Context A/73/310/Rev.1 (September 19, 2018).

7. Informal settlements range from constantly displaced homeless encampments in the most affluent countries, to massive communities in the global South, such as Orangi Town in Karachi, Pakistan, with an estimated 2.4 million inhabitants. . . .

26. The right to remain in one's home and community is central to the right to housing. . . .

28. The right to in situ upgrading must be recognized in law and communities should be provided with representation to seek enforcement of this right. Barrio Rodrigo Bueno in Buenos Aires, visited by the Special Rapporteur in 2016, has been successful in this respect. Situated in the midst of commercial and luxury residential developments, the community successfully contested applications for eviction and won the right to in situ upgrading. Legislation has recently been enacted which provides for the upgrading of the community with ongoing communication with and collaboration of residents. . . .

29. States should immediately cease and desist from seeking to justify evictions of residents of informal settlements under domestic legal procedures. Courts should refuse to authorize such evictions in any but the most exceptional circumstances, and only when residents have been fully engaged in the process, when alternative housing of comparable or better quality is being provided and when all other requirements of international human rights have been honoured. Applications to evict are almost always indicative of flawed processes and lack of meaningful engagement with communities.

30. The approach taken by the South African courts moves in the right direction and should be applied by other courts. In the *Melani* case, the Slovo Park informal settlement challenged the decision of the City of Johannesburg not to apply for in situ upgrading and instead to relocate the community to an alternative location 11 km away. The court held that the Government's upgrading policy, as required by the constitutional right to housing, envisages "a holistic development approach with minimum disruption or distortion of existing fragile community networks and support structures and encourages engagement between local authorities and residents living within informal settlements". Relocation must be "the exception and not the rule" and any relocation must be to a location "as close as possible to the existing settlement". On this basis, the City was ordered to reverse the decision to relocate the community and apply for funding for in situ upgrading. . . .

39. Planning and zoning should never be used to justify unwarranted demolition of informal settlements, to deny access to services or to prevent relocation to proximate lands. In Lagos, Nigeria, the Urban and Regional Planning and Development Law of 2010 retroactively granted powers to authorities to seal up and demolish structures that contravened Lagos planning laws, resulting in the demolition of the informal settlement of Makoko, which housed approximately 85,000 people. . . .

105. It is unfortunately common for police, security forces and other hired personnel to use force and violence, including with weapons, when informal settlement residents resist forced eviction or are otherwise claiming their right to housing through protest.

106. Those who resist forced eviction and claim their right to housing must be treated as human rights defenders by government authorities and security forces and the international community should respond accordingly when their rights are violated. If police or security personnel are required to use force for other reasons, the principles of necessity and proportionality need to be respected and they must conduct their operations in line with human rights standards, respecting and protecting the rights of informal settlement residents and their property. Where excessive force is used against informal settlement residents, the situation must be referred to an independent and impartial panel for investigation and remedy.

e.   Global Migration

On December 10 and 11, the United Nations approved a non-binding cooperative framework negotiated in July 2018 to improve coordination of responses to migration of large groups of people globally.[48] The Compact is in part a response to a human migration crisis arising due to political instabilities in places including Syria, Yemen, and Venezuela. As of 2018, approximately 258 million people are on the move including 124.8 million women and 36.1 million children.[49] Disturbingly in 2018, for the fifth consecutive year, more than 3000 people have either died or gone missing on migratory routes. A newly established network on migration coordinated by the International Organization for Migration supports implementation of the Compact. The following excerpt from the Compact highlights the shared objectives of States adopting the Compact.

GLOBAL COMPACT FOR SAFE, ORDERLY AND REGULAR MIGRATION (13 JULY 2018)

With the New York Declaration for Refugees and Migrants we adopted a political declaration and a set of commitments. Reaffirming that Declaration in its entirety, we build upon it by laying out the following cooperative framework comprised of 23 objectives, implementation, as well as follow-up and review. . . .

(1) Collect and utilize accurate and disaggregated data as a basis for evidence-based policies
(2) Minimize the adverse drivers and structural factors that compel people to leave their country of origin
(3) Provide accurate and timely information at all stages of migration

48. Global Compact for Safe, Orderly and Regular Migration https://refugeesmigrants. un.org/sites/default/files/180713_agreed_outcome_global_compact_for_migration.pdf.
49. International Organization of Migration, Global Migration Indicators 2018 http:// publications.iom.int/system/files/pdf/global_migration_indicators_2018.pdf.

(4) Ensure that all migrants have proof of legal identity and adequate documentation

(5) Enhance availability and flexibility of pathways for regular migration

(6) Facilitate fair and ethical recruitment and safeguard conditions that ensure decent work

(7) Address and reduce vulnerabilities in migration

(8) Save lives and establish coordinated international efforts on missing migrants

(9) Strengthen the transnational response to smuggling of migrants

(10) Prevent, combat and eradicate trafficking in persons in the context of international migration

(11) Manage borders in an integrated, secure and coordinated manner

(12) Strengthen certainty and predictability in migration procedures for appropriate screening, assessment and referral

(13) Use migration detention only as a measure of last resort and work towards alternatives

(14) Enhance consular protection, assistance and cooperation throughout the migration cycle

(15) Provide access to basic services for migrants

(16) Empower migrants and societies to realize full inclusion and social cohesion

(17) Eliminate all forms of discrimination and promote evidence-based public discourse to shape perceptions of migration

(18) Invest in skills development and facilitate mutual recognition of skills, qualifications and competences

(19) Create conditions for migrants and diasporas to fully contribute to sustainable development in all countries

(20) Promote faster, safer and cheaper transfer of remittances and foster financial inclusion of migrants

(21) Cooperate in facilitating safe and dignified return and readmission, as well as sustainable reintegration

(22) Establish mechanisms for the portability of social security entitlements and earned benefits

(23) Strengthen international cooperation and global partnerships for safe, orderly and regular migration

f.   Business and Human Rights

In 2018, the open-ended intergovernmental working group on transnational corporations and other business enterprises with respect to human rights prepared a zero-draft for negotiation by the 90 States attending the work group. The document will continue to be negotiated in 2019 with a new draft to be presented in June 2019 that may address some of the concerns of States raised in 2018 including the need for an enforcement mechanism. This treaty negotiation builds directly off the work of John Ruggie when he served as UN Secretary-General's Special Representative for Business and Human Rights and promoted a UN Framework and

Guiding Principles that articulated (1) the State duty to protect against human rights abuses by third parties, including business; (2) the corporate responsibility to respect human rights; and (3) the need to give victims of human rights abuses greater access to effective remedies.[50] The 2018 working draft of the proposed human rights treaty follows.[51]

LEGALLY BINDING INSTRUMENT TO REGULATE IN INTERNATIONAL HUMAN RIGHTS LAW THE ACTIVITIES OF TRANSNATIONAL CORPORATIONS AND OTHER BUSINESS ENTERPRISES

[Article 1 which includes Preamble is omitted]

ARTICLE 2.   STATEMENT OF PURPOSE

The purpose of this Convention is to:

To strengthen the respect, promotion, protection and fulfilment of human rights in the context of business activities of transnational character;

To ensure an effective access to justice and remedy to victims of human rights violations in the context of business activities of transnational character, and to prevent the occurrence of such violations;

To advance international cooperation with a view towards fulfilling States' obligations under international human rights law;

ARTICLE 3.   SCOPE

1. This Convention shall apply to human rights violations in the context of any business activities of a transnational character.

2. This Convention shall cover all international human rights and those rights recognized under domestic law.

ARTICLE 4.   DEFINITIONS

1. "Victims" shall mean persons who individually or collectively alleged to have suffered harm, including physical or mental injury, emotional suffering, economic loss or substantial impairment of their human rights, including environmental rights, through acts or omissions in the context of

50. John Ruggie, Framework and Guiding Principles (2008) http://www.reports-and-materials .org/Ruggie-report-7-Apr-2008.pdf
51. Available at https://www.ohchr.org/Documents/HRBodies/HRCouncil/WGTransCorp/ Session3/DraftLBI.pdf.

business activities of a transnational character. Where appropriate, and in accordance with domestic law, the term "victim" also includes the immediate family or dependents of the direct victim and persons who have suffered harm in intervening to assist victims in distress or to prevent victimization.

2. "Business activities of a transnational character" shall mean any for-profit economic activity, including but not limited to productive or commercial activity, undertaken by a natural or legal person, including activities undertaken by electronic means, that take place or involve actions, persons or impact in two or more national jurisdictions.

ARTICLE 5.   JURISDICTION

1. Jurisdiction, with respect to actions brought by an individual or group of individuals, independently of their nationality or place of domicile, arising from acts or omissions that result in violations of human rights covered under this Convention, shall vest in the court of the State where:

> a. such acts or omissions occurred or;
> b. the Court of the State where the natural or legal person or association of natural or legal persons alleged to have committed the acts or omissions are domiciled.

2. A legal person or association of natural or legal persons is considered domiciled at the place where it has its:
> a. statutory seat, or
> b. central administration, or
> c. substantial business interest, or
> d. subsidiary, agency, instrumentality, branch, representative office or the like.

3. Where a claim is submitted on behalf of an individual or group of individuals, this shall be with their consent unless the claimant can justify acting on their behalf without consent.

ARTICLE 6.   STATUTE OF LIMITATIONS

1. Statutes of limitations shall not apply to violations of international human rights law which constitute crimes under international law. Domestic statutes of limitations for other types of violations that do not constitute crimes under international law, including those time limitations applicable to civil claims and other procedures, should not be unduly restrictive and shall allow an adequate period of time for the investigation and prosecution of the violation, particularly in cases where the violations occurred abroad.

ARTICLE 7.   APPLICABLE LAW

1. Subject to the following paragraph, all matters of substance or procedure regarding claims before the competent court which are not specifically regulated in the Convention shall be governed by the law of that court, including any rules of such law relating to conflict of laws.

2. At the request of victims, all matters of substance regarding human rights law relevant to claims before the competent court may be governed by the law of another Party where the involved person with business activities of a transnational character is domiciled. The competent court may request for mutual legal assistance as referred to under Article 11 of this Convention.

3. The Convention does not prejudge the recognition and protection of any rights of victims that may be provided under applicable domestic law.

ARTICLE 8.   RIGHTS OF VICTIMS

1. Victims shall have the right to fair, effective and prompt access to justice and remedies in accordance with international law. Such remedies shall include, but shall not be limited to:

> a. Restitution, compensation, rehabilitation, satisfaction and guarantees of non-repetition for victims.
> b. Environmental remediation and ecological restoration where applicable, including covering of expenses for relocation of victims, and replacement of community facilities.

2. State Parties shall guarantee the right of victims, individually or as a group, to present claims to their Courts, and shall provide their domestic judicial and other competent authorities with the necessary jurisdiction in accordance with this Convention in order to allow for victim's access to adequate, timely and effective remedies.

3. States Parties shall investigate all human rights violations effectively, promptly, thoroughly and impartially and, where appropriate, take action against those natural or legal persons allegedly responsible, in accordance with domestic and international law.

4. Victims shall be guaranteed appropriate access to information relevant to the pursuit of remedies. State parties shall ensure that their domestic laws and Courts do not unduly limit such right, and facilitate access to information through international cooperation, as set out in this Convention, and in line with confidentiality rules under domestic law.

5. States shall provide proper and effective legal assistance to victims throughout the legal process, including by:

> a. Informing victims of their procedural rights and the scope, timing and progress of their claims in an opportune and adequate manner;
>
> b. Guaranteeing the rights of victims to be heard in all stages of proceedings without prejudice to the accused and consistent with the relevant domestic law;
>
> c. Avoiding unnecessary formalities, costs or delay for bringing a claim and during the disposition of cases and the execution of orders or decrees granting awards to victims;
>
> d. Providing assistance with all procedural requirements for the presentation of a claim and the start and continuation of proceedings in the courts of that State Party. The State Party concerned shall determine the need for legal assistance, in full consultation with the victims, taking into consideration the economic resources available to the victim, the complexity and length of the issues involved proceedings. In no case shall victims be required to reimburse any legal expenses of the other party to the claim.

6. Inability to cover administrative and other costs shall not be a barrier to commencing proceedings in accordance with this Convention. States shall assist victims in overcoming such barriers, including through waiving costs where needed. States shall not require victims to provide a warranty as a condition for commencing proceedings.

7. States Parties shall establish an International Fund for Victims covered under this Convention, to provide legal and financial aid to victims. This Fund shall be established at most after (X) years of the entry into force of this Convention. The Conference of Parties shall define and establish the relevant provisions for the functioning of the Fund.

8. States shall provide effective mechanisms for the enforcement of remedies, including national or foreign judgments, in accordance with the present Convention, domestic law and international legal obligations.

9. Victims shall have access to appropriate diplomatic and consular means, as needed, to ensure that they can exercise their right to access justice and remedies, including, but not limited to, access to information required to bring a claim, legal aid and information on the location and competence of the courts and the way in which proceedings are commenced or defended before those courts.

10. Victims shall be treated with humanity and respect for their dignity and human rights, and their safety, physical and psychological well-being and privacy shall be ensured.

11. States shall protect victims, their representatives, families and witnesses from any unlawful interference with their privacy and from intimidation, and retaliation, before, during and after any proceedings have been instituted.

12. States shall guarantee the right to life, personal integrity, freedom of opinion and expression, peaceful assembly and association, and free movement of victims, their representatives, families and victims.

13. Victims shall have the right to benefit from special consideration and care to avoid revictimization in the course of proceedings for access to justice and remedies.

ARTICLE 9.   PREVENTION

1. State Parties shall ensure in their domestic legislation that all persons with business activities of transnational character within such State Parties' territory or otherwise under their jurisdiction or control shall undertake due diligence obligations throughout such business activities, taking into consideration the potential impact on human rights resulting from the size, nature, context of and risk associated with the business activities.

2. Due diligence referred to above under Article 7.1 shall include, but shall not be necessarily limited to:

> a. Monitoring the human rights impact of its business activities including the activities of its subsidiaries and that of entities under its direct or indirect control or directly linked to its operations, products or services.
> b. Identify and assess any actual or potential human rights violations that may arise through their own activities including that of their subsidiaries and of entities under their direct or indirect control or directly linked to its operations, products or services.
> c. Prevent human rights violations within the context of its business activities, including the activities of its subsidiaries and that of entities under its direct or indirect control or directly linked to its operations, products or services, including through financial contribution where needed.
> d. Reporting publicly and periodically on non-financial matters, including at a minimum environmental and human rights matters, including policies, risks, outcomes and indicators. The requirement to disclose this information should be subject to an assessment of the severity of the potential impacts on the individuals and communities concerned, not to a consideration of their materiality to the financial interests of the business or its shareholders.
> e. Undertaking pre and post environmental and human rights impact assessments covering its activities and that of its subsidiaries and

entities under its control, and integrating the findings across relevant internal functions and processes and taking appropriate action.

f. Reflecting the requirements in paragraphs a. to e. above in all contractual relationships which involve business activities of transnational character.

g. Carrying out meaningful consultations with groups whose human rights are potentially affected by the business activities and other relevant stakeholders, through appropriate procedures including through their representative institutions, while giving special attention to those facing heightened risks of violations of human rights within the context of business activities, such as women, children, persons with disabilities, indigenous peoples, migrants, refugees and internal displaced persons.

h. Due diligence may require establishing and maintaining financial security, such as insurance bonds or other financial guarantees to cover potential claims of compensation.

3. State Parties shall ensure that effective national procedures are in place to enforce compliance with the obligations laid down under this article, and that those procedures are available to all natural and and legal persons having a legitimate interest, in accordance with national law, in ensuring that the article is respected.

4. Failure to comply with due diligence duties under this article shall result in commensurate liability and compensation in accordance with the articles of this Convention.

5. States Parties may elect to exempt certain small and medium-sized undertakings from the purview of selected obligations under this article with the aim of not causing undue additional administrative burdens.

ARTICLE 10. LEGAL LIABILITY

1. State Parties shall ensure through their domestic law that natural and legal persons may be held criminally, civil or administratively liable for violations of human rights undertaken in the context of business activities of transnational character. Such liability shall be subject to effective, proportionate, and dissuasive criminal and non-criminal sanctions, including monetary sanctions. Liability of legal persons shall be without prejudice to the liability of natural persons.

2. Civil liability shall not be made contingent upon finding of criminal liability or its equivalent for the same actor.

3. Where a person with business activities of a transnational character is found liable for reparation to a victim, such party shall provide reparation

to the victim or compensate the State if the State has already provided reparation to the victim.

4. Subject to domestic law, courts asserting jurisdiction under this Convention may require, where needed, reversal of the burden of proof for the purpose of fulfilling the victim's access to justice.

CIVIL LIABILITY

5. State Parties shall provide for a comprehensive regime of civil liability for violations of human rights undertaken in the context of business activities and for fair, adequate and prompt compensation.

State Parties shall ensure that effective national procedures are in place to enforce compliance

6. All persons with business activities of a transnational character shall be liable for harm caused by violations of human rights arising in the context of their business activities, including throughout their operations:

> a. to the extent it exercises control over the operations, or
> b. to the extent it exhibits a sufficiently close relation with its subsidiary or entity in its supply chain and where there is strong and direct connection between its conduct and the wrong suffered by the victim, or
> c. to the extent risk have been foreseen or should have been foreseen of human rights violations within its chain of economic activity.

7. Civil liability of legal persons shall be independent from any criminal procedure against that entity.

CRIMINAL LIABILITY

8. State Parties shall provide measures under domestic law to establish criminal liability for all persons with business activities of a transnational character that intentionally, whether directly or through intermediaries, commit human rights violations that amount to a criminal offence, including crimes recognized under international law , international human rights instruments, or domestic legislation. Such criminal liability for human rights violations that amount to a criminal offence, shall apply to principals, accomplices and accessories, as may be defined by domestic law.

9. Criminal liability of legal persons shall be without prejudice to the criminal liability of the natural persons who have committed the offences.

10. Each State Party shall, in particular, ensure that legal persons held liable in accordance with this article are subject to effective, proportionate and dissuasive criminal or non-criminal sanctions, including monetary sanctions.

11. Where applicable under international law, States shall incorporate or otherwise implement within their domestic law appropriate provisions for universal jurisdiction over human rights violations that amount to crimes.

12. In the event that, under the legal system of a Party, criminal responsibility is not applicable to legal persons, that Party shall ensure that legal persons shall be subject to effective, proportionate and dissuasive non-criminal sanctions, including monetary sanctions or other administrative sanctions, for acts covered under the previous two paragraphs.

ARTICLE 11.   MUTUAL LEGAL ASSISTANCE

1. States Parties shall cooperate in good faith to enable the implementation of commitments under this Convention and the fulfillment of the purposes of this Convention.

2. States Parties shall afford one another the widest measure of mutual legal assistance in initiating and carrying out investigations, prosecutions and judicial proceedings in relation to the cases covered by this Convention, including access to information and supply of all evidence at their disposal and necessary for the proceedings in order to allow effective, prompt, thorough and impartial investigations covered under this Convention. The requested Party shall inform the requesting Party, as soon as possible, of any additional information or documents needed to support the request for assistance and, where requested, of the status and outcome of the request for assistance. The requesting State Party may require that the requested State Party keep confidential the fact and substance of the request, except to the extent necessary to execute the request.

3. Mutual legal assistance under this Convention is understood to include, but is not limited to:

   a. Taking evidence or statements from persons;
   b. Effecting service of judicial documents;
   c. Executing searches and seizures;
   d. Examining objects and sites;
   e. Providing information, evidentiary items and expert evaluations;
   f. Providing originals or certified copies of relevant documents and records, including government, bank, financial, corporate or business records;
   g. Identifying or tracing proceeds of crime, property, instrumentalities or other things for evidentiary purposes;
   h. Facilitating the voluntary appearance of persons in the requesting State Party;
   i. Facilitating the freezing and recovery of assets;

j. Assistance to, and protection of, victims, their families, representatives and witnesses, consistent with international human rights legal standards and subject to international legal requirements including those relating to the prohibition of torture and other forms of cruel, inhuman or degrading treatment or punishment;

k. Assistance in regard to application and interpretation of human rights law;

l. Any other type of assistance that is not contrary to the domestic law of the requested State Party.

4. Without prejudice to domestic law, the competent authorities of a State Party may, without prior request, transmit information relating to criminal matters covered under this Convention to a competent authority in another State Party where they believe that such information could assist the authority in undertaking or successfully concluding inquiries and criminal proceedings or could result in a request formulated by the latter State Party pursuant to this Convention. The transmission of information shall be without prejudice to inquiries and criminal proceedings in the State of the competent authorities providing the information.

5. States Parties shall consider concluding bilateral or multilateral agreements or arrangements whereby, in relation to matters that are subject of investigations, prosecutions or judicial proceedings under this Convention, the competent authorities concerned may establish joint investigative bodies. In the absence of such agreements or arrangements, joint investigations may be undertaken by agreement on a case-by-case basis. The States Parties involved shall ensure that the sovereignty of the State Party in whose territory such investigation is to take place, is fully respected.

6. States Parties shall carry out their obligations under the previous Article in conformity with any treaties or other arrangements on mutual legal assistance that may exist between them. In the absence of such treaties or arrangements, States Parties shall afford one another assistance in a way not contrary to domestic law.

7. In accordance with domestic systems, each State Party shall designate a central authority that shall have the responsibility and power to receive requests for mutual legal assistance and either to execute them or to transmit them to the competent authorities for execution.

8. State Parties shall provide judicial assistance and other forms of cooperation in the pursuit of access to remedy for victims of human rights violations covered under this Convention.

9. Any judgment of a court having jurisdiction in accordance with this Convention which is enforceable in the State of origin of the judgment and is no longer subject to ordinary forms of review shall be recognized

and enforced in any Party as soon as the formalities required in that Party have been completed, whereby formalities should not be more onerous and fees and charges should not be higher than those required for the enforcement of domestic judgments and shall not permit the re-opening of the merits of the case.

10. Recognition and enforcement may be refused, at the request of the defendant, only if that party furnishes to the competent authority where the recognition and enforcement is sought, proof that (a) the defendant was not given reasonable notice and a fair opportunity to present his or her case; (b) where the judgment is irreconcilable with an earlier judgment validly pronounced in another Party with regard to the same cause of action and the same parties; or (c) where the judgment is contrary to the public policy of the Party in which its recognition is sought.

11. Mutual legal assistance under this article may be refused by a State Party if the violation to which the request relates is not covered by this Convention or if it would be contrary to the legal system of the requested State Party.

12. A Party shall not decline to render mutual legal assistance for criminal matters within the scope of this Convention on the ground of bank secrecy. . . .

[Article 13 on Consistency of International Law, Article 14 on Institutional Arrangements, and Article 15 on Final Provisions omitted.]

VIII.   Immunities

Sovereign immunity is the legal doctrine that prevents a court from adjudicating certain matters that involve a State in either a civil action or a criminal proceeding. Diplomatic immunity may also be extended to certain State representatives. There are a variety of ways that a State might approach an immunity case. This section will summarize two U.S. cases involving sovereign immunity and one case involving diplomatic immunity.

a.   State Immunity

In the United States, the Supreme Court decided on February 21, 2018 in *Rubin v. Islamic Republic of Iran* that victims of terrorism violence could not acquire Iranian antiquities held by the University of Chicago without violating the Foreign Sovereign Immunities Act (FSIA).[52] The plaintiffs in

---

52. Rubin v. Islamic Republic of Iran, 583 U.S. ___ (2018).

attempting to satisfy a U.S. $71.5 million default judgment against Iran were unable to rely on the FSIA because the Supreme Court was unwilling to read a "terrorism exception" into § 1610(g) of the act. The following excerpt provides a summary of the decision:

> Petitioners hold a judgment against respondent Islamic Republic of Iran pursuant to one such exception to jurisdictional immunity, which applies where the foreign state is designated as a state sponsor of terrorism and the claims arise out of acts of terrorism. See §1605A. The issue presented in this case is whether certain property of Iran, specifically, a collection of antiquities owned by Iran but in the possession of respondent University of Chicago, is subject to attachment and execution by petitioners in satisfaction of that judgment. Petitioners contend that the property is stripped of its immunity by another provision of the FSIA, §1610(g), which they maintain provides a blanket exception to the immunity typically afforded to the property of a foreign state where the party seeking to attach and execute holds a §1605A judgment.

> We disagree. Section 1610(g) serves to identify property that will be available for attachment and execution in satisfaction of a §1605A judgment, but it does not in itself divest property of immunity. Rather, the provision's language "as provided in this section" shows that §1610(g) operates only when the property at issue is exempt from immunity as provided elsewhere in §1610. Petitioners cannot invoke §1610(g) to attach and execute against the antiquities at issue here, which petitioners have not established are exempt from immunity under any other provision in §1610.

> Section 1610(g) conspicuously lacks the textual markers, "shall not be immune" or "notwithstanding any other provision of law," that would have shown that it serves as an independent avenue for abrogation of immunity. In fact, its use of the phrase "as provided in this section" signals the opposite: A judgment holder seeking to take advantage of §1610(g)(1) must identify a basis under one of §1610's express immunity-abrogating provisions to attach and execute against a relevant property."

One additional case may be of interest to international practitioners: *Republic of Sudan v. Harrison*, 138 S. Ct. 2671 (2018), was argued in November 2018. The question for the Supreme court was whether the U.S. Court of Appeals for the 2nd Circuit erred by holding—in direct conflict with the U.S. Courts of Appeals for the District of Columbia, 5th Circuit, and 7th Circuit and in the face of an amicus brief from the United States—that plaintiffs suing a foreign state under the Foreign Sovereign Immunities Act may serve the foreign state under 28 U.S.C. § 1608(a)(3) by mail addressed and dispatched to the head of the foreign state's ministry of foreign affairs "via" or in "care of" the foreign state's diplomatic mission in the United States, despite U.S. obligations under the Vienna Convention on Diplomatic Relations. The background for the case involved the service of a summons and complaint by the clerk of the court on behalf of the sailors and spouses of sailors injured in the 2000 bombing of the U.S.S. Cole in the Port of Aden, Yemen. The documents were served on the Minister of Foreign Affairs of Sudan via the Sudanese Embassy in Washington, D.C., and a return receipt was received. When Sudan did not answer the complaint within the required time frame, the clerk of the court entered a default judgment against Sudan that was the basis for the U.S. District Court for the Southern District of New York issuing several bank turnover orders. Sudan finally made an appearance leading to the current case.[53]

b.   Diplomatic Immunity

In August 2018, the High Court of South Africa issued an opinion denying diplomatic immunity to the first lady of Zimbabwe.[54] The case was brought by three South African women who alleged they were mentally and physically attacked by Dr. Grace Mugabe in a South African hotel room. The police department investigated a criminal charge, and the government of Zimbabwe indicated it would be invoking diplomatic immunity because Dr. Mugabe was part of the South African Development Community summit. The Court had to decide whether Dr. Mugabe was entitled to diplomatic immunity for the alleged unlawful act perpetrated against South African nationals by virtue of being a spouse of a head of state. If she was not, the Court had to decide whether the decision of the South African government to confer or grant immunity to Dr. Mugabe was constitutional and lawful. After a discussion of customary international law and concluding that customary international law does not have a rule requiring a recognition of diplomatic immunity for family members of a head of State, the court ultimately rejected immunity.

IX.   *Emerging International Legal Issues*

a.   Cyberattacks

A topic that is attracting international legal attention is the increase in cyberattacks alleged to have been launched by States. What is the state responsibility and liability associated with an attack such as a ransomware allegedly launched from North Korea that impacted a major U.S. law

---

53. On March 26, 2019, the Supreme Court decided in a 8-1 decision that notice needed to be provided to Sudan's foreign ministry in Khartoum. Service on Sudan's embassy in Washington was not sufficient under the Foreign Sovereign Immunities Act.

54. Gabriella Engels v. SA Govt. & Grace Mugabe (August 4, 2018) http://politicsweb.co.za/documents/gabriella-engels-vs-sa-govt--grace-mugabe-high-cou.

firm? There is no specific legal framework for addressing cyberattacks. Some practitioners suggest that the existing Law of War including the UN Charter's Article 2.4 prohibiting aggression should be applied to any cyberattack that proximately results in death, injury, or significant destruction. Most thinking about cyberattacks continues to apply the traditional law of war treaties and principles such as necessity and proportionality. Some businesses including Microsoft have called for a "digital Geneva Convention."[55]

At least one State has outlined its policy on cyberattacks and international law. The following excerpt is from a British keynote by the Attorney General.[56]

"[E]very state should be clear about the legal principles and thresholds it believes apply in cyberspace and I want to be as clear as I can be about the UK's position. . . . First, there is the rule prohibiting interventions in the domestic affairs of states both under Article 2(7) of the Charter and in customary international law. This prohibition means that any activity in cyber space which reaches the level of such an intervention is unlawful. Any activity of this nature by a state could only become permissible in response to some prior illegality by another state.

The next relevant provision of the UN Charter is in Article 2(4) which prohibits the threat or use of force against the territorial independence or political integrity of any state. Any activity above this threshold would only be lawful under the usual exceptions—when taken in response to an armed attack in self-defence or as a Chapter VII action authorised by the Security Council. In addition, the UK remains of the view that it is permitted under international law, in exceptional circumstances, to use force on the grounds of humanitarian intervention to avert an overwhelming humanitarian catastrophe.

Thirdly, the UK considers it is clear that cyber operations that result in, or present an imminent threat of, death and destruction on an equivalent scale to an armed attack will give rise to an inherent right to take action in self-defence, as recognised in Article 51 of the UN Charter.

If a hostile state interferes with the operation of one of our nuclear reactors, resulting in widespread loss of life, the fact that the act is carried out by way of a cyber operation does not prevent it from being viewed as an unlawful use of force or an armed attack against us. If it would be a breach of international law to bomb an air traffic control tower with the effect of downing civilian aircraft, then it will be a breach of international law to use a hostile cyber operation to disable air traffic control systems which results in the same, ultimately lethal, effects.

55. A Digital Geneva Convention to Protect Cyberspace https://query.prod.cms. rt.microsoft.com/cms/api/am/binary/RW67QH.
56. UK Attorney General Jeremy Wright, Cyber and International Law in the 21st Century (May 23, 2018) https://www.gov.uk/government/speeches/cyber-and-international-law-in-the-21st-century.

Acts like the targeting of essential medical services are no less prohibited interventions, or even armed attacks, when they are committed by cyber means.

And in addition to the provisions of the UN Charter, the application of international humanitarian law to cyber operations in armed conflicts provides both protection and clarity. When states are engaged in an armed conflict, this means that cyber operations can be used to hinder the ability of hostile groups . . . to coordinate attacks, and in order to protect coalition forces on the battlefield. But like other responsible states, this also means that even on the new battlefields of cyber space, the UK considers that there is an existing body of principles and rules that seek to minimise the humanitarian consequences of conflict. . . .

The international law prohibition on intervention in the internal affairs of other states is of particular importance in modern times when technology has an increasing role to play in every facet of our lives, including political campaigns and the conduct of elections. As set out by the International Court of Justice in its judgment in the Nicaragua case, the purpose of this principle is to ensure that all states remain free from external, coercive intervention in the matters of government which are at the heart of a state's sovereignty, such as the freedom to choose its own political, social, economic and cultural system.

The precise boundaries of this principle are the subject of ongoing debate between states, and not just in the context of cyber space. But the practical application of the principle in this context would be the use by a hostile state of cyber operations to manipulate the electoral system to alter the results of an election in another state, intervention in the fundamental operation of Parliament, or in the stability of our financial system. Such acts must surely be a breach of the prohibition on intervention in the domestic affairs of states. . . .

Countermeasures cannot involve the use of force, and they must be both necessary and proportionate to the purpose of inducing the hostile state to comply with its obligations under international law. . . .

These restrictions under the doctrine of countermeasures are generally accepted across the international law community. The one area where the UK departs from the excellent work of the International Law Commission on this issue is where the UK is responding to covert cyber intrusion with countermeasures.

In such circumstances, we would not agree that we are always legally obliged to give prior notification to the hostile state before taking countermeasures against it. The covertness and secrecy of the countermeasures must of course be considered necessary and proportionate to the original illegality, but we say it could not be right for international law to require a countermeasure to expose highly sensitive capabilities in defending the country in the cyber arena, as in any other arena.

In addition, it is also worth stating that, as a matter of law, there is no requirement in the doctrine of countermeasures for a response to be symmetrical to the underlying unlawful act. What matters is necessity and proportionality, which means that the UK could respond to a cyber intrusion through non-cyber means, and vice versa. . . .

The international law rules on the attribution of conduct to a state are clear, set out in the International Law Commissions Articles on State Responsibility, and require a state to bear responsibility in international law for its internationally wrongful acts, and also for the acts of individuals acting under its instruction, direction or control.

These principles must be adapted and applied to a densely technical world of electronic signatures, hard to trace networks and the dark web. They must be applied to situations in which the actions of states are masked, often deliberately, by the involvement of non-state actors. And international law is clear - states cannot escape accountability under the law simply by the involvement of such proxy actors acting under their direction and control . . . But for all the work I have described, both domestic and international, it remains the case that defining the appropriate principles of international law to apply to cyberspace is difficult.

b. Artificial Intelligence, Weapon Systems, and Legal Responsibility

With the rise of "smart machines" that may be deployed during armed conflict, there is an increasing interest in what legal regime should be applied when disputes arise. There are ongoing debates about whether existing responsibility and liability models are appropriate. Civil society actors have called for a robust international dialogue about the social implications of using artificial intelligence systems. In December 2018, the University of Montreal opened the "Montreal Declaration on the Responsible Development of Artificial Intelligence" for signature by global actors. Whether this civil society declaration leads to State action remains to be seen, but Principle 9 is legally relevant with signatories acknowledging that "[t]he development and use of artificial intelligence systems must not contribute to lessen the responsibility of human beings when decisions must be made."[57]

Of particular concern is the interaction between artificial intelligence and humanitarian law. While there has been debate over the use of surveillance drones, the new developments in weapon systems with autonomous capacities to deploy lethal forces raise a new set of pressing ethical and legal questions. China, the United States, and Russia are developing these types of capabilities. Technology experts and civil society

---

57. Montreal Declaration for a responsible development of artificial intelligence (2018) https://docs.wixstatic.com/ugd/ebc3a3_c5c1c196fc164756afb92466c081d7ae.pdf.

groups encourage a strong application of the precautionary principle in advancing artificial intelligence capabilities in the context of preparing for war. At least one civil society group has called for a ban through an international treaty on the use of fully autonomous lethal weapons.[58] Legal scholars call for "meaningful human control" over any weapon systems being developed that incorporate artificial intelligence. Some of the core issues in the field are nicely highlighted by Ted Piccone writing for the Brookings Institution:[59]

> At the heart of this debate is the concept that these highly automated systems must have "meaningful human control" to comply with humanitarian legal requirements such as distinction, proportionality, and precautions against attacks on civilians. Where should responsibility for errors of design and use lie in the spectrum between 1) the software engineers writing the code that tells a weapons system when and against whom to target an attack, 2) the operators in the field who carry out such attacks, and 3) the commanders who supervise them? How can testing and verification of increasingly autonomous weapons be handled in a way that will create enough transparency, and some level of confidence, to reach international agreements to avoid worst-case scenarios of mutual destruction?

> Beyond the legal questions, experts in this field are grappling with a host of operational problems that impinge directly on matters of responsibility for legal and ethical design. First, military commanders and personnel must know if an automated weapon system is reliable and predictable in its relevant functions. Machine learning, by its nature, cannot guarantee what will happen when an advanced autonomous system encounters a new situation, including how it will interact with other highly autonomous systems. Second, the ability of machines to differentiate between combatants and civilians must overcome inherent biases in how visual and audio recognition features operate in real time. Third, the ability of computers not just to collect data but to analyze and interpret them correctly is another open question.

> The creation of distributed "systems of systems" connected through remote cloud computing further complicates how to assign responsibility for attacks that go awry. Given the commercial availability of sophisticated technology at relatively low cost, the ease of hacking, deceit, and other countermeasures by state and non-state actors is another major concern. Ultimately, as AI is deployed to maximize the advantage of speed in fighting comparably equipped militaries, we may enter a new era of "hyperwar" where humans in the loop create more rather than fewer vulnerabilities to the ultimate warfighting aim.

---

58. Campaign to Stop Killer Robots, https://www.stopkillerrobots.org/learn/#solution.
59. Ted Piccone, How Can International Law Regulate Autonomous Weapons? (April 10, 2018) https://www.brookings.edu/blog/order-from-chaos/2018/04/10/how-can-international-law-regulate-autonomous-weapons/.

c.   International Environmental Law and Global Warming

The topic of the acceleration of global warming touches on many aspects of international law ranging from health to human security to borders. In 2018, the global message from the Intergovernmental Panel on Climate Change in its special report on global warming was unequivocal.[60] Impacts of a global increase in temperature have already been observed on natural and human systems. Future climate-related risks will depend on the rate, peak, and duration of warming. The report indicated that greenhouse-gas pollution needs to be cut in half in the next 12 years and then fall to zero by 2050. To limit warming to 2 °C, emissions will need to fall to zero by 2075. The United States along with Saudi Arabia, Kuwait, and Russia opposed a proposal at the 2018 Conference of Parties to endorse the recommendation study from the UN Intergovernmental Panel on Climate Change.

International courts have continued to be the site of climate change related adjudications. In December 2018, the European Court of Justice decided that the European Commission was not allowed to change the limits of nitrogen oxides for vehicles after establishing a standard.[61] In 2007, the EU set a new engine class—Euro 6—for diesel engines with a limit of 80 mg of nitrogen oxides (NOx) per km. In 2016, the Commission relaxed its standards, allowing the new engines to produce more than double the target. What this means in practice is that Brussels, Paris, and Madrid do not have to permit certain vehicles unless the vehicles can meet a stricter standard.

Civil society groups have prevailed in two significant cases. In 2018, the Hague Court of Appeal in the Netherlands upheld the 2015 decision of the District Court in the *Urgenda* case ordering the Dutch Government to reduce its greenhouse gas emissions by 25% by 2020 compared to 1990 levels.[62] The Dutch government appealed the decision.

In April 2018, the Colombian Supreme Court delivered a significant decision in support of national action to end deforestation to protect the climate on behalf of Colombian youth between the ages of 7 and 25.[63] The following is a translation from the plaintiffs of key portions of the decision

60. Intergovernmental Panel on Climate Change in its special report on global warming https://www.ipcc.ch/sr15/

61. European Court of Justice, Judgment in Cases T-339/16 Ville de Paris v Commission, T-352/16 Ville de Bruxelles v Commission, T- 391/16 Ville de Madrid v Commission (December 13, 2018)

62. Gerechtshof Den Haag, State must achieve higher reduction in greenhouse gas emissions in short term (October 9, 2018) https://www.rechtspraak.nl/Organisatie-en-contact/ Organisatie/Gerechtshoven/Gerechtshof-Den-Haag/Nieuws/Paginas/State-must-achieve-higher-reduction-in-greenhouse-gas-emissions-in-short-term.aspx.

63. Excerpts from Dejusticia case to stop deforestation before Colombia Supreme Court (Corte Suprema de Justicia, Sala de Casación Civil) on behalf of 25 Colombian youth (April 4, 2018) https://cdn.dejusticia.org/wp-content/uploads/2018/04/Tutela-English-Excerpts-1.pdf.

and is quoted at length because of the significance of this decision in recognizing intergenerational rights, applying the precautionary principle, and articulating the principle of solidarity.

1. The plaintiffs plead for the protection of "supralegal" rights, highlighting those of "enjoying a healthy environment," life, and health, allegedly violated by the accused.

2. They argue as a basis for their claim, in summary, the following:

2.1. As a first measure, they are identified as

"(. . .) a group of 25 children, adolescents, and young adults . . . between 7 and 25 years of age, living in cities that are part of the list of cities most at risk due to climate change. . . . [With] a hope to live for 78 years on average (75 years for men and 80 for women) which is why they expect to develop their adult life between 2041-2017 [sic] and in their old age from 2071 onwards. In those periods of time, according to the climate change scenarios presented by IDEAM,[64] the average temperature in Colombia is expected to increase by 1.6°C and 2.14°C, respectively. (. . .)"

2.2 They explain that in the Paris Agreement and in Law 1753 of 2015, the government acquired national and international commitments to achieve ". . . *reduction of deforestation and the emission of greenhouse gases in a context of climate change* . . ." among which, the obligation to "reduce the net rate of deforestation to zero in the Colombian Amazon by 2020" stands out. . . .

We are all obligated to stop exclusively thinking about our self-interest. We must consider the way in which our daily actions and behaviors affect society and nature. In the words of Peces-Barba, we must shift from "private ethics," focused on private goods, to "public ethics," understood as the implementation of moral values that aim to achieve a particular notion of social justice. . . .

5.2 The protection of fundamental rights not only involves the individual, but implicates the "other." The neighbor is otherness; its essence, the other people that inhabit the planet, also include other animal and plant species. But in addition, this includes the unborn, who also deserve to enjoy the same environmental conditions that we have.

5.3 The environmental rights of future generations are based on the (i) ethical duty of the solidarity of the species and (ii) on the intrinsic value of nature. . . .

The factors reviewed directly generate deforestation in the Amazon, causing short, medium, and long term imminent and serious damage to the children, adolescents and adults who filed this lawsuit, and in general, all inhabitants of the national territory, including both present and future generations, as it leads to rampant emissions of carbon dioxide (CO_2) into the atmosphere, producing the greenhouse gas effect, which in turn transforms and fragments

64. IDEAM is an acronym for Institute of Hydrology, Meterology and the Environment. It is an agency of the Ministry of Environment and Sustainable Development in Colombia.

ecosystems, altering water sources and the water supply for population centers and land degradation. . . .

This previous reality, in contrast with the legal environmental principles of i) precaution; intergenerational equity; and (iii) solidarity, leads the Court to conclude the following:

11.1 Relative to the first of the aforementioned principles, there is no doubt that there is a risk of damage, given that according to the IDEAM, the increase in GHG emissions resulting from deforestation in the Amazon forest would generate an increase in Colombia's temperature between "*0.7 and 1.1 degrees Celsius between 2011 and 2040*," while for the period "*between 2041 and 2070*", the estimates indicate an increase between "*1.4 and 1.7*" degrees Celsius, to reach 2.7 degrees Celsius "*in the period between 2071 and 2100*."

Likewise, the mass reduction of the Amazon forest would break the ecosystem connection with the Andes, causing the probable extinction or threat of the subsistence of species inhabiting that corridor, generating "*damage in its ecological integrity.*"

Additionally, according to the IDEAM, GHG emissions due to deforestation would result in two main types of consequences related to rainfall. First, an increase in several regions of the country, a situation that would trigger an increase in water levels and thus, in runoff, spreading polluting agents coming from water. Second, a deficit in other departments, causing a reduction in the water supply, as well as prolonged droughts.

The irreversibility of the damage and the scientific certainty, both additional components of the precautionary principle, are also evident since the GHG emitted from deforestation, constitutes 36% of the forestry sector, rapidly becoming an uncontrollable component of CO2 emissions; information supported, in detail, by the studies conducted by the IDEAM, the Ministry of Foreign Affairs, the Ministry of Environment and Sustainable Development, the UNDP, and many others.

11.2 In terms of intergenerational equity, the transgression is obvious, as the forecast of temperature increase is 1.6 degrees in 2041 and 2.14 in 2071; future generations, including children who brought this action, will be directly affected, unless we presently reduce the deforestation rate to zero.

11.3 The principle of solidarity, for the specific case, is determined by the duty and co-responsibility of the Colombian state to stop the causes of the GHG emissions from the abrupt forest reduction in the Amazon; thus, it is imperative to adopt immediate mitigation measures, and to protect the right to environmental welfare, both of the plaintiffs, and to the other people who inhabit and share the Amazonian territory, not only nationals, but foreigners, together with all inhabitants of the globe, including ecosystems and living beings.

The previous reality, in addition to transgressing the regulations pertaining to the Environmental Charter of the country, and the international instruments that make up the global ecological public order, constitutes a serious ignorance of the obligations acquired by the State in the Framework Convention on Climate Change of Paris 2015, where Colombia, among other commitments, undertook an agreement to reduce the "*deforestation in the Colombian Amazon*," with the objective of reducing deforestation to zero in that region by 2020, as achieving it, according to the Ministry of Environment and Sustainable Development, would ensure that ". . . 44 megatons of greenhouse gases would not enter the atmosphere and 100,000 hectares of agriculture in areas of high deforestation would be more friendly to the environment . . . ."

It is up to the authorities to respond effectively to the specific questions of the problem, among which, it is important to highlight the urgent need to adopt mitigation and corrective measures for i) the excessive expansion of illicit crops and illegal mining that unreasonably destroy the Amazonian forest; ii) fill the void left by the FARC and paramilitaries to make an active state presence in favor of the conservation of Amazonian territories that in the context of armed conflict were conquered by insurgent groups, merciless predators, irrational colonizers, and generally, people and organizations outside the law; iii) prevent and mitigate the growing fires, deforestation, and unreasonable expansion of the agricultural frontier; iv) the lack of prevention of the consequences inherent to constructing roads, granting titles to property and mining concessions; v) the expansion of large-scale agroindustrial and livestock farming; vi) the preservation of this ecosystem due to its importance in regulating the global climate; vii) the lack of scientific calculations of the release of tons of carbon through burning and the loss of biomass, which constitutes the vegetation cover; and viii) to confront climate change due to the destruction of the Amazon rainforest in the national territory.

12. Therefore, the excessive intensification of this problem is evident, showing the ineffectiveness of governmental measures adopted to confront this, and, from that perspective, granting the protection for the breach of fundamental guarantees to water, air, a dignified life, health, among others in connection with the environment.

14. Therefore, in order to protect this ecosystem vital for our global future, just as the Constitutional Court declared the Atrato river, the Colombian Amazon is recognized as a "subject of rights," entitled to protection, conservation, maintenance and restoration led by the State and the territorial agencies.

Consequently, we grant the relief, and order the Presidency of the Republic, the Ministry of Environment and Sustainable Development, and the Ministry of Agriculture and Rural Development, in coordination with the actors of the National Environmental System and the participation of the plaintiffs, the affected communities, and the interested population in general, to formulate a short, medium, and long term action plan within the next four (4) months from today's notice, to counteract the rate of deforestation in the Amazon, tackling climate change impacts.

This plan will aim to mitigate the early deforestation warnings issued by the IDEAM.

Likewise, the Presidency of the Republic, the Ministry of Environment and Sustainable Development, and the Ministry of Agriculture and Rural

Development, will be ordered to formulate within the next five months following today's notice, with the active participation of the plaintiffs, the affected communities, scientific organizations or environmental research groups, and the interested population in general, the construction of an **"intergenerational pact for the life of the Colombian Amazon—PIVAC"** to adopt measures aimed at reducing deforestation to zero and greenhouse gas emissions, and has national, regional, and local implementation strategies of a preventative, mandatory, corrective, and pedagogical nature, directed towards climate change adaptation.

Also, all the municipalities of the Colombian Amazon, within the next five months following today's notice, are compelled to update and implement the Land Management Plans, and when relevant, include an action plan to reduce deforestation to zero in its territory, which should encompass preventative, mandatory, corrective, and pedagogical measurable strategies, oriented towards climate change adaptation.

Building on some of the momentum of the success in the *Urgenda* case and the decision by the Colombian Supreme Court, several additional international lawsuits have been filed against governments. These lawsuits include:

<u>France</u>—On December 17, 2018, four nonprofits sent a "lettre préalable indemnitaire" (letter of formal notice) to the French Prime Minister and other government representatives to begin the first stage in a legal proceeding against the French government for inadequate action on climate change.[65]

<u>Germany</u>—On October 25, 2018, three organic farming families in Germany filed a lawsuit against the German government alleging that the government's failure to meet its 2020 climate target is a violation of the families' rights to life and health.[66] In 2007, the German government pledged to cut its emissions by 40 percent below 1990 levels by 2020 but has since indicated that it will not be able to meet these targets.

Globally we need to reach and sustain "net-zero" carbon dioxide emissions if we hope to reverse existing warming trends. This will not be an easy task especially with trends indicating that emissions from the U.S., the

65. Notre Affaire a Tous, Greenpeace, Fondation Pour La Nature et L'Homme, and Oxfam, Letter of Formal Notice to Officials (December 19, 2018) http://blogs2.law.columbia.edu/climate-change-litigation/wp-content/uploads/sites/16/non-us-case-documents/2018/20181217_NA_na-1.pdf.

66. Greenpeace e.V., vertreten durch den Vorstand (Roland Hipp, Sweelin Heuss und Martin Kaiser) (October 25, 2018) http://blogs2.law.columbia.edu/climate-change-litigation/wp-content/uploads/sites/16/non-us-case-documents/2018/20181025_Not-Yet-Available_complaint.pdf.

world's second largest greenhouse gas emitter, rose sharply in 2018.[67] The concept and practice of "law" is never addressed in the report, but it is clear that if we are to collectively reduce carbon emissions in a world of global communication and trade that States will need to coordinate governance responses.

––––––––––––––

For any questions or comments about materials in this Updates and Commentary in Public International Law, please email Anastasia Telesetsky at atelesetsky@uidaho.edu.

67. Chris Mooney and Brady Dennis, U.S. greenhouse gas emissions spiked in 2018—and it couldn't happen at a worse time (January 8, 2019) https://www.washingtonpost.com/ national/health-science/us-greenhouse-gas-emissions-spiked-in-2018–and-it-couldnt-happen-at-a-worse-time/2019/01/07/68cff792-12d6-11e9-803c-4ef28312c8b9_story.html?utm_term=. a9f590762fab.

www.ingramcontent.com/pod-product-compliance
Lightning Source LLC
Chambersburg PA
CBHW061838220326
41599CB00027B/5333